The Tao of Pooh
&
The Te of Piglet

Winnie-the-Pooh has a way of doing things, which has made him the world's most beloved bear. And Pooh's way, as Benjamin Hoff brilliantly demonstrates, seems strangely close to the ancient principles of Taoist Philosophy. Hesitant Piglet exhibits a very important principle of Taoism: the *Te*- a Chinese word meaning virtue of the small.

Benjamin Hoff's explanations of Taoism and Te through Pooh and Piglet show that this is not an ancient and remote philosophy, but something you can use here and now. And that is a Very Useful Thing to Know.

Benjamin Hoff is an American writer, photographer, musician and composer. He writes full time and practises Taoist Yoga and T'ai Chi Chu'an in his spare time. He lives in Portland, Oregon.

BENJAMIN HOFF

The Tao of Pooh
&
The Te of Piglet

with illustrations by E. H. Shepard

METHUEN

The Tao of Pooh first published in Great Britain 1982 by Methuen Children's Books
The Te of Piglet first published in Great Britain 1992 by Methuen London
Combined edition first published in Great Britain 1994 by Methuen London
This paperback edition first published 1998 by Methuen Children's Books
an imprint of Egmont Children's Books Limited
239 Kensington High Street, London W8 6SA

Text by A. A. Milne and line illustrations by E. H. Shepard from *Winnie-the-Pooh*
and *The House at Pooh Corner* copyright under the Berne Convention
Grateful acknowledgement is made to the Trustees of the Pooh Properties for use
of the quoted material by A. A. Milne and the line illustrations by E. H. Shepard.

Hope against Hope: A Memoir by Nadezhda Mandelstam,
translated from the Russian by Max Hayward
with an introduction by Clarence Brown. (Atheneum Publishers, 1970).
Land of the Spotted Eagle by Luther Standing Bear. Copyright © 1933
by Luther Standing Bear. Renewal copyright © 1960 by May Jones.
Magical Child by Joseph Chilton Pearce.
Copyright © 1977 by Joseph Chilton Pearce.
Selected Prose 1909-1965 by Ezra Pound (London: Faber 1973).
Copyright © 1973 by the Estate of Ezra Pound.
Reprinted by kind permission of Faber & Faber Ltd.
Dickens by Peter Ackroyd (London: Sinclair Stevenson, 1990).
Copyright © 1990 by Peter Ackroyd.
The Life of Mahatma Gandhi by Louis Fischer
(London: Jonathan Cape, 1951). Copyright © 1951 by Louis Fischer.

A CIP catalogue record for this title is available from the British Library

5 7 9 10 8 6 4

ISBN 0 416 19526 1

Printed and bound in Great Britain by Cox & Wyman Ltd, Reading, Berkshire

The Tao of Pooh

For Han Hsiang-tse

Cottleston, Cottleston, Cottleston Pie,
A fly can't bird, but a bird can fly.
Ask me a riddle and I reply:
"*Cottleston, Cottleston, Cottleston Pie.*"

Contents

Foreword

"What's this you're writing?" asked Pooh, climbing onto the writing table.

"The Tao of Pooh," I replied.

"The *how* of Pooh?" asked Pooh, smudging one of the words I had just written.

"The *Tao* of Pooh," I replied, poking his paw away with my pencil.

"It seems more like the *ow!* of Pooh," said Pooh, rubbing his paw.

"Well, it's not," I replied huffily.

"What's it about?" asked Pooh, leaning forward and smearing another word.

"It's about how to stay happy and calm under all circumstances!" I yelled.

"Have you read it?" asked Pooh.

That was after some of us were discussing the Great Masters of Wisdom, and someone was saying how all of them came from the East, and I was saying that some of them didn't, but he was going on and on, just like this sentence, not paying any attention, when I decided to read a quotation of Wisdom from the West, to prove that there was more to the world than one half, and I read:

> "When you wake up in the morning, Pooh," said Piglet at last, "what's the first thing you say to yourself?"
>
> "What's for breakfast?" said Pooh. "What do *you* say, Piglet?"
>
> "I say, I wonder what's going to happen exciting *today*?" said Piglet.
>
> Pooh nodded thoughtfully.
>
> "It's the same thing," he said.

"What's that?" the Unbeliever asked.

"Wisdom from a Western Taoist," I said.

"It sounds like something from *Winnie-the-Pooh*," he said.

"It is," I said.

"That's not about Taoism," he said.

"Oh, yes it is," I said.

"No, it's not," he said.

"What do you think it's about?" I said.

"It's about this dumpy little bear that wanders around asking silly questions, making up songs, and going through all kinds of adventures, without ever accumulating any amount of intellectual knowledge or losing his simpleminded sort of happiness. *That's* what it's about," he said.

"Same thing," I said.

That was when I began to get an idea: to write a book that explained the principles of Taoism through Winnie-the-Pooh, and explained Winnie-the-Pooh through the principles of Taoism.

When informed of my intentions, the scholars exclaimed, "Pre*pos*terous!" and things like that. Others said it was the stupidest thing they'd ever heard, and that I must be dreaming. Some said it was a nice idea, but too difficult. "Just where would you even begin?" they asked. Well, an old Taoist saying puts it this way: "A thousand-mile journey starts with one step."

So I think that we will start at the beginning . . .

The *How* of Pooh?

"You see, Pooh," I said, "a lot of people don't seem to know what Taoism is . . ."

"Yes?" said Pooh, blinking his eyes.

"So that's what this chapter is for — to explain things a bit."

"Oh, I see," said Pooh.

"And the easiest way to do that would be for us to go to China for a moment."

"*What?*" said Pooh, his eyes wide open in amazement. "Right now?"

"Of course. All we need to do is lean back, relax, and there we are."

"Oh, I see," said Pooh.

Let's imagine that we have walked down a narrow

street in a large Chinese city and have found a small shop that sells scrolls painted in the classic manner. We go inside and ask to be shown something allegorical – something humorous, perhaps, but with some sort of Timeless Meaning. The shopkeeper smiles. "I have just the thing," he tells us. "A copy of *The Vinegar Tasters!*" He leads us to a large table and unrolls the scroll, placing it down for us to examine. "Excuse me – I must attend to something for a moment," he says, and goes into the back of the shop, leaving us alone with the painting.

Although we can see that this is a fairly recent version, we know that the original was painted long ago; just when is uncertain. But by now, the theme of the painting is well known.

We see three men standing around a vat of vinegar. Each has dipped his finger into the vinegar and has tasted it. The expression on each man's face shows his individual reaction. Since the painting is allegorical, we are to understand that these are no ordinary vinegar tasters, but are instead representatives of the "Three Teachings" of China, and that the vinegar they are sampling represents the Essence of Life. The three masters are K'ung Fu-tse (Confucius), Buddha, and Lao-tse, author of the oldest existing book of Taoism. The first has a sour look on his face, the second wears a bitter expression, but the third man is smiling.

To K'ung Fu-tse (kung FOOdsuh), life seemed rather sour. He believed that the present was out of step with the past, and that the government of man on earth was out of harmony with the Way of Heaven, the government of the universe. Therefore, he emphasized reverence for the Ancestors, as well as for the ancient rituals and ceremonies in which the emperor, as the Son of Heaven, acted as intermediary between limitless heaven and limited earth. Under Confucianism, the use of precisely measured court music, prescribed steps, actions, and phrases all added up to an extremely complex system of rituals, each used for a particular purpose at a particular time. A saying was recorded about K'ung Fu-tse: "If the mat was not straight, the Master would not sit." This ought to give an indication of the extent to which things were carried out under Confucianism.

To Buddha, the second figure in the painting, life on earth was bitter, filled with attachments and desires that led to suffering. The world was seen as a setter of traps, a generator of illusions, a revolving wheel of pain for all creatures. In order to find peace, the Buddhist considered it necessary to transcend "the world of dust" and reach Nirvana, literally a state of "no wind." Although the essentially optimistic attitude of the Chinese altered Buddhism considerably after it was brought in from its native India, the devout Buddhist often saw the way to Nirvana interrupted all the same by the bitter wind of everyday existence.

To Lao-tse (LAOdsuh), the harmony that naturally existed between heaven and earth from the very beginning could be found by anyone at any time, but not by following the rules of the Confucianists. As he stated in his *Tao Te Ching* (DAO DEH JEENG), the "Tao Virtue Book," earth was in essence a reflection of heaven, run by the same laws — *not* by the laws of men. These laws affected not only the spinning of distant planets, but the activities of the birds in the forest and the fish in the sea. According to Lao-tse, the more man interfered with the natural balance produced and governed by the universal laws, the further away the harmony retreated into the distance. The more forcing, the more trouble. Whether heavy or light, wet or dry, fast or slow, everything had its own nature already within it, which could not be violated without causing difficulties. When abstract and arbitrary rules were imposed from the outside, struggle was inevitable. Only then did life become sour.

To Lao-tse, the world was not a setter of traps but a teacher of valuable lessons. Its lessons needed to be learned, just as its laws needed to be followed; then all would go well. Rather than turn away from "the world of dust," Lao-tse advised others to "join the dust of the world." What he saw operating behind everything in heaven and earth he called *Tao* (DAO), "the Way." A basic principle of Lao-tse's teaching was that this Way of the Universe could not be adequately described in words, and that it would be insulting both to its unlimited power and to the intelligent human mind to attempt to do so. Still, its nature could be understood, and those who cared the most about it, and the life from which it was inseparable, understood it best.

Over the centuries Lao-tse's classic teachings were developed and divided into philosophical, monastic, and folk religious forms. All of these could be included under the general heading of Taoism. But the basic Taoism that we are concerned with here is simply a particular way of appreciating, learning from, and working with whatever happens in everyday life. From the Taoist point of view, the natural result of this harmonious way of living is happiness. You might say that happy serenity is the most noticeable characteristic of the Taoist personality, and a subtle sense of humor is apparent even in the most profound Taoist writings, such as the twenty-five-hundred-year-old *Tao Te Ching*. In the writings of Taoism's second major writer, Chuang-tse (JUANGdsuh), quiet laughter seems to bubble up like water from a fountain.

"But what does that have to do with vinegar?" asked Pooh.

"I thought I had explained that," I said.

"I don't think so," said Pooh.

"Well, then, I'll explain it now."

"That's good," said Pooh.

In the painting, why is Lao-tse smiling? After all, that vinegar that represents life must certainly have an unpleasant taste, as the expressions on the faces of the other two men indicate. But, through working in harmony with life's circumstances, Taoist understanding changes what others may perceive as negative into something positive. From the Taoist point of view, sourness and bitterness come from the interfering and unappreciative mind. Life itself, when understood and utilized for what it is, is sweet. That is the message of *The Vinegar Tasters*.

"Sweet? You mean like honey?" asked Pooh.

"Well, maybe not *that* sweet," I said. "That would be overdoing it a bit."

"Are we still supposed to be in China?" Pooh asked cautiously.

"No, we're through explaining and now we're back at the writing table."

"Oh."

"Well, we're just in time for a little something," he added, wandering over to the kitchen cupboard.

The Tao of *Who?*

We were discussing the definition of wisdom late one night, and we were just about to fall asleep from it all when Pooh remarked that his understanding of Taoist principles had been passed down to him from certain Ancient Ancestors.

"Like who?" I asked.

"Like Pooh Tao-tse, the famous Chinese painter," Pooh said.

"That's *Wu* Tao-tse."

"Or how about Li Pooh, the famous Taoist poet?" Pooh asked cautiously.

"You mean Li *Po*," I said.

"Oh," said Pooh, looking down at his feet.

Then I thought of something. "That doesn't really

matter, anyway," I said, "because one of the most important principles of Taoism was named after you."

"Really?" Pooh asked, looking more hopeful.

"Of course — *P'u*, the Uncarved Block."

"I'd forgotten," said Pooh.

So here we are, about to try to explain *P'u*, the Uncarved Block. In the classic Taoist manner, we won't try too hard or explain too much, because that would only Confuse things, and because it would leave the impression that it was all only an intellectual idea that could be left on the intellectual level and ignored. Then you could say, "Well, this idea is all very nice, but what does it amount to?" So instead, we will try to *show* what it amounts to, in various ways.

P'u, by the way, is pronounced sort of like Pooh, but without so much *oo* — like the sound you make when blowing a fly off your arm on a hot summer day.

Before we bring our Resident Expert in for a few illuminating remarks, let's explain something.

The essence of the principle of the Uncarved Block is that things in their original simplicity contain their own natural power, power that is easily spoiled and lost when that simplicity is changed. For the written character *P'u*, the typical Chinese dictionary will give a definition of "natural, simple, plain, honest."

P'u is composed of two separate characters combined: the first, the "radical" or root-meaning one, is that for tree or wood; the second, the "phonetic" or sound-giving one, is the character for dense growth or thicket. So from "tree in a thicket" or "wood not cut" comes the meaning of "things in their natural state" – what is generally represented in English versions of Taoist writing as the "uncarved block."

This basic Taoist principle applies not only to *things* in their natural beauty and function, but to people as well. Or Bears. Which brings us to Pooh, the very Epitome of the Uncarved Block. As an illustration of the principle, he may appear a bit *too* simple at times . . .

> "I *think* it's more to the right," said Piglet nervously. "What do *you* think, Pooh?"

> Pooh looked at his two paws. He knew that one of them was the right, and he knew that when

you had decided which one of them was the
right, then the other one was the left, but he
never could remember how to begin.

"Well," he said slowly . . .

. . . but, no matter how he may seem to others,
especially to those fooled by appearances, Pooh, the
Uncarved Block, is able to accomplish what he does
because he *is* simpleminded. As any old Taoist walking
out of the woods can tell you, simpleminded does
not necessarily mean *stupid*. It's rather significant that
the Taoist ideal is that of the still, calm, reflecting
"mirror-mind" of the Uncarved Block, and it's rather
significant that Pooh, rather than the thinkers Rabbit,
Owl, or Eeyore, is the true hero of *Winnie-the-Pooh*
and *The House at Pooh Corner.*

"The fact is," said Rabbit, "we've missed our way
somehow."

They were having a rest in a small sand-pit on
the top of the Forest. Pooh was getting rather
tired of that sand-pit, and suspected it of following
them about, because whichever direction they
started in, they always ended up at it, and each
time, as it came through the mist at them, Rabbit
said triumphantly, "Now I know where we are!"
and Pooh said sadly, "So do I," and Piglet said

nothing. He had tried to think of something to say, but the only thing he could think of was, "Help, help!" and it seemed silly to say that, when he had Pooh and Rabbit with him.

"Well," said Rabbit, after a long silence in which nobody thanked him for the nice walk they were having, "we'd better get on, I suppose. Which way shall we try?"

"How would it be," said Pooh slowly, "if, as soon as we're out of sight of this Pit, we try to find it again?"

"What's the good of that?" said Rabbit.

"Well," said Pooh, "we keep looking for Home and not finding it, so I thought that if we looked for this Pit, we'd be sure not to find it, which would be a Good Thing, because then we might find something that we *weren't* looking for, which might be just what we *were* looking for, really."

"I don't see much sense in that," said Rabbit . . .

"If I walked away from this Pit, and then walked back to it, of *course* I should find it."

"Well, I thought perhaps you wouldn't," said Pooh. "I just thought."

"Try," said Piglet suddenly. "We'll wait here for you."

Rabbit gave a laugh to show how silly Piglet

was, and walked into the mist. After he had gone a hundred yards, he turned and walked back again . . . and after Pooh and Piglet had waited twenty minutes for him, Pooh got up.

"I just thought," said Pooh. "Now then, Piglet, let's go home."

"But, Pooh," cried Piglet, all excited, "do you know the way?"

"No," said Pooh. "But there are twelve pots of honey in my cupboard, and they've been calling to me for hours. I couldn't hear them properly before, because Rabbit *would* talk, but if nobody says anything except those twelve pots, I *think*, Piglet, I shall know where they're calling from. Come on."

They walked off together; and for a long time Piglet said nothing, so as not to interrupt the pots; and then suddenly he made a squeaky noise . . . and an oo-noise . . . because now he began to know where he was; but he still didn't dare to say so out loud, in case he wasn't. And just when he was getting so sure of himself that it didn't matter whether the pots went on calling or not, there was a shout in front of them, and out of the mist came Christopher Robin.

After all, if it were Cleverness that counted most, Rabbit would be Number One, instead of that Bear.

But that's not the way things work.

> "We've come to wish you a Very Happy Thursday," said Pooh, when he had gone in and out once or twice just to make sure that he *could* get out again.
>
> "Why, what's going to happen on Thursday?" asked Rabbit, and when Pooh had explained, and Rabbit, whose life was made up of Important Things, said, "Oh, I thought you'd really come about something," they sat down for a little . . . and by-and-by Pooh and Piglet went on again. The wind was behind them now, so they didn't have to shout.
>
> "Rabbit's clever," said Pooh thoughtfully.
>
> "Yes," said Piglet, "Rabbit's clever."
>
> "And he has Brain."
>
> "Yes," said Piglet, "Rabbit has Brain."
>
> There was a long silence.
>
> "I suppose," said Pooh, "that that's why he never understands anything."

And if Clever Rabbit doesn't quite have what it takes, Abrasive Eeyore certainly doesn't either. Why not? Because of what we could call the Eeyore Attitude. You might say that while Rabbit's little routine is that of Knowledge for the sake of Being Clever, and while Owl's is that of Knowledge for the sake of Appearing Wise, Eeyore's is Knowledge for the sake of Complaining About Something. As anyone who doesn't have it can see, the Eeyore Attitude gets in the way of things like wisdom and happiness, and pretty much prevents any sort of real Accomplishment in life:

> Eeyore, the old grey Donkey, stood by the side of the stream, and looked at himself in the water.
>
> "Pathetic," he said. "That's what it is. Pathetic."
>
> He turned and walked slowly down the stream for twenty yards, splashed across it, and walked slowly back on the other side. Then he looked at himself in the water again.
>
> "As I thought," he said. "No better from *this* side. But nobody minds. Nobody cares. Pathetic, that's what it is."
>
> There was a crackling noise in the bracken behind him, and out came Pooh.
>
> "Good morning, Eeyore," said Pooh.
>
> "Good morning, Pooh Bear," said Eeyore gloomily. "If it *is* a good morning," he said. "Which I doubt," said he.
>
> "Why, what's the matter?"

"Nothing, Pooh Bear, nothing. We can't all, and some of us don't. That's all there is to it."

It's not that the Eeyore Attitude is necessarily without a certain severe sort of humor . . .

"Hallo, Eeyore," they called out cheerfully.

"Ah!" said Eeyore. "Lost your way?"

"We just came to see you," said Piglet. "And to see how your house was. Look, Pooh, it's still standing!"

"I know," said Eeyore. "Very odd. Somebody ought to have come down and pushed it over."

"We wondered whether the wind would blow it down," said Pooh.

"Ah, that's why nobody's bothered, I suppose. I thought perhaps they'd forgotten."

. . . it's just that it's really not so awfully much *fun.*

Not like a few other points of view we can think of.
A little too complex or something. After all, what is
it about *Pooh* that makes him so lovable?

"Well, to begin with . . ." said Pooh.

. . . Yes, well, to begin with, we have the principle
of the Uncarved Block. After all, what is the most
appealing thing about Pooh? What else but —

"Well, to begin with . . ."

. . . simplicity, the Simplicity of the Uncarved
Block? And the nicest thing about that Simplicity is
its useful wisdom, the what-is-there-to-eat variety —
wisdom you can get at.

Considering that, let's have *Pooh* describe the
nature of the Uncarved Block.

"All right, Pooh, what can you tell us about the
Uncarved Block?"

"The *what?*" asked Pooh, sitting up suddenly and
opening his eyes.

"The Uncarved Block. *You* know. . ."

"Oh, the . . . Oh."

"What do you have to say about it?"

"I didn't do it," said Pooh.

"You – "

"It must have been Piglet," he said.

"I did not!" squeaked Piglet.

"Oh, Piglet. Where did *you* – "

"I *didn't*," Piglet said.

"Well, then, it was probably Rabbit," said Pooh.

"It wasn't *me!*" Piglet insisted.

"Did someone call?" said Rabbit, popping up from behind a chair.

"Oh – Rabbit," I said. "We're talking about the Uncarved Block."

"Haven't seen it," said Rabbit, "but I'll go ask Owl."

"That won't be nec – ," I began.

"Too late now," said Pooh. "He's gone."

"I never even *heard* of the Uncarved Block," said Piglet.

"Neither did I," said Pooh, rubbing his ear.

"It's just a figure of speech," I said.

"A what of a *who?*" asked Pooh.

"A figure of speech. It means that, well, the Uncarved Block is a way of saying, 'like Pooh.' "

"Oh, is *that* all?" said Piglet.

"I wondered," said Pooh.

Pooh can't describe the Uncarved Block to us in words; he just *is* it. *That's* the nature of the Uncarved Block.

"A perfect description. Thank you, Pooh."
"Not at all," said Pooh.

When you discard arrogance, complexity, and a few other things that get in the way, sooner or later you will discover that simple, childlike, and mysterious secret known to those of the Uncarved Block: Life is Fun.

> Now one autumn morning when the wind had blown all the leaves off the trees in the night, and was trying to blow the branches off, Pooh and Piglet were sitting in the Thoughtful Spot and wondering.
>
> "What *I* think," said Pooh, "is I think we'll go to Pooh Corner and see Eeyore, because perhaps his house has been blown down, and perhaps he'd like us to build it again."
>
> "What *I* think," said Piglet, "is I think we'll go and see Christopher Robin, only he won't be there, so we can't."
>
> "Let's go and see *everybody*," said Pooh. "Because when you've been walking in the wind for miles, and you suddenly go into somebody's house, and he says, 'Hallo, Pooh, you're just in time for a little smackerel of something,' and you are, then it's what I call a Friendly Day."

Piglet thought that they ought to have a Reason
for going to see everybody, like Looking for Small
or Organizing an Expotition, if Pooh could think
of something.

Pooh could.

"We'll go because it's Thursday," he said, "and
we'll go to wish everybody a Very Happy Thursday. Come on, Piglet."

From the state of the Uncarved Block comes the
ability to enjoy the simple and the quiet, the natural
and the plain. Along with that comes the ability to
do things spontaneously and have them work, odd as
that may appear to others at times. As Piglet put it in
Winnie-the-Pooh, "Pooh hasn't much Brain, but he
never comes to any harm. He does silly things and
they turn out right."

To understand all this a little better, it might help
to look at someone who is quite the opposite —
someone like, well, say, *Owl* for example . . .

Spelling Tuesday

Through copse and spinney marched Bear; down open slopes of gorse and heather, over rocky beds of streams, up steep banks of sandstone into the heather again; and so at last, tired and hungry, to the Hundred Acre Wood. For it was in the Hundred Acre Wood that Owl lived.

"And if anyone knows anything about anything," said Bear to himself, "it's Owl who knows something about something," he said, "or my name's not Winnie-the-Pooh," he said. "Which it is," he added. "So there you are."

So now we come to Owl's house, as some of us have so many times before, searching for answers to questions of one sort or another. Will we find the answers here?

Before we go in and take a look around, it seems appropriate to have a few Background Remarks about the kind of scholar that Owl represents, in relation to the attitudes and principles of Taoism that we are concerned with here.

To begin with, it is necessary to point out that in China, scholars were generally Confucianist in training and orientation, and therefore often spoke a somewhat different language from the Taoists, who tended to see Confucianist scholars as busy ants spoiling the picnic of life, rushing back and forth to pick up the bits and pieces dropped from above. In the final section of the *Tao Te Ching*, Lao-tse wrote, "The wise are not learned; the learned are not wise" – an attitude shared by countless Taoists before and since.

From the Taoist point of view, while the scholarly intellect may be useful for analyzing certain things, deeper and broader matters are beyond its limited reach. The Taoist writer Chuang-tse worded it this way:

> A well-frog cannot imagine the ocean, nor can a summer insect conceive of ice. How then can a scholar understand the Tao? He is restricted by his own learning.

(This and other selections from classic oriental texts are my own translations and adaptations.)

It seems rather odd, somehow, that Taoism, the way of the Whole Man, the True Man, the Spirit Man (to use a few Taoist terms), is for the most part interpreted here in the West by the Scholarly Owl – by the Brain, the Academician, the dry-as-dust Absentminded Professor. Far from reflecting the Taoist ideal of wholeness and independence, this incomplete and unbalanced creature divides all kinds of abstract things into little categories and compartments, while remaining rather helpless and disorganized in his daily life. Rather than learn from Taoist teachers and from direct experience, he learns intellectually and indirectly, from books. And since he doesn't usually put Taoist principles into practice in an everyday sort of way, his explanations of them tend to leave out some rather important details, such as how they work and where you can apply them.

On top of that, it is very hard to find any of the *spirit* of Taoism in the lifeless writings of the humorless Academic Mortician, whose bleached-out Scholarly Dissertations contain no more of the character of Taoist wisdom than does the typical wax museum.

But that is the sort of thing we can expect from the Abstract Owl, the dried-up Western descendant of the Confucianist Dedicated Scholar, who, unlike his Noble but rather Unimaginative ancestor, thinks he has some sort of monopoly on –

"What's *that?*" Pooh interrupted.

"What's *what?*" I asked.

"What you just said – the Confusionist, Desiccated Scholar."

"Well, let's see. The Confusionist, Desiccated Scholar is one who studies Knowledge for the sake of Knowledge, and who keeps what he learns to himself or to his own small group, writing pompous and pretentious papers that no one else can understand, rather than working for the enlightenment of others. How's that?"

"Much better," said Pooh.

"Owl is about to illustrate the Confusionist, Desiccated Scholar," I said.

"I see," said Pooh.

Which brings us back to Owl. Let's see — how did Rabbit describe the situation with Owl? Oh, here it is:

> . . . you can't help respecting anybody who can spell TUESDAY, even if he doesn't spell it right; but spelling isn't everything. There are days when spelling Tuesday simply doesn't count.

"By the way, Pooh, how do *you* spell Tuesday?"

"Spell what?" asked Pooh.

"Tuesday. You know — Monday, Tuesday . . ."

"My dear Pooh," said Owl, "*everybody* knows that it's spelled with a *Two*."

"Is it?" asked Pooh.

"Of course," said Owl. "After all, it's the second day of the week."

"Oh, is *that* the way it works?" asked Pooh.

"All right, Owl," I said. "Then what comes after Twosday?"

"*Thirdsday*," said Owl.

"Owl, you're just confusing things," I said. "This is the day after Tuesday, and it's not Thirds — I mean, *Thursday*."

"Then what is it?" asked Owl.
"It's *Today!*" squeaked Piglet.
"My favorite day," said Pooh.

Ours, too. We wonder why the scholars don't think much of it. Perhaps it's because they Confuse themselves thinking about other days so much.

Now one rather annoying thing about scholars is that they are always using Big Words that some of us can't understand . . .

> "Well," said Owl, "the customary procedure in such cases is as follows."
>
> "What does Crustimoney Proseedcake mean?" said Pooh. "For I am a Bear of Very Little Brain, and long words Bother me."
>
> "It means the Thing to Do."
>
> "As long as it means that, I don't mind," said Pooh humbly.

. . . and one sometimes gets the impression that those intimidating words are there to *keep* us from understanding. That way, the scholars can appear Superior, and will not likely be suspected of Not Knowing Something. After all, from the scholarly point of view, it's practically a crime not to know everything.

But sometimes the knowledge of the scholar is a bit hard to understand because it doesn't seem to match up with our own experience of things. In other words, Knowledge and Experience do not necessarily speak the same language. But isn't the knowledge that comes from experience more valuable than the knowledge that doesn't? It seems fairly obvious to some of us that a lot of scholars need to go outside and sniff around – walk through the grass, talk to the animals. That sort of thing.

"Lots of people talk to animals," said Pooh.
"Maybe, but . . ."
"Not very many *listen*, though," he said.
"That's the problem," he added.

In other words, you might say that there is more to Knowing than just being correct. As the mystical poet Han-shan wrote:

A scholar named Wang
Laughed at my poems.
The accents are wrong,
He said,
Too many beats;
The meter is poor,
The wording impulsive.

I laugh at his poems,
As he laughs at mine.
They read like
The words of a blind man
Describing the sun.

Quite often, struggling like a scholar over relatively
unimportant matters can make one increasingly
Confused. Pooh described the Confusionist's state of
mind quite accurately:

On Monday, when the sun is hot,
I wonder to myself a lot:
"Now is it true, or is it not,
That what is which and which is what?"

On Tuesday, when it hails and snows,
The feeling on me grows and grows
That hardly anybody knows
If those are these or these are those.

On Wednesday, when the sky is blue,
And I have nothing else to do,
I sometimes wonder if it's true
That who is what and what is who.

On Thursday, when it starts to freeze,
And hoar-frost twinkles on the trees,
How very readily one sees
That these are whose — but whose are these?

On Friday . . .

Yes, whose *are* these, anyway? To the Desiccated Scholars, putting names on things is the most vital activity in the world. *Tree. Flower. Dog.* But don't ask them to prune the tree, plant the flower, or take care of the dog, unless you enjoy Unpleasant Surprises. Living, growing things are beyond them, it seems.

Now, scholars can be very useful and necessary, in their own dull and unamusing way. They provide a lot of information. It's just that there is Something More, and that Something More is what life is really all about.

Oops. "Say, Pooh, have you seen my other pencil?"

"I saw Owl using it a little while ago," said Pooh.

"Oh, here it is. What's this? 'Aardvarks and Their Aberrations.' "

"Beg pardon?" said Pooh.

" 'Aardvarks and Their Aberrations' – what Owl was writing about."

"Oh, were they?" said Pooh.

"Say, this pencil's all chewed up."

One more funny thing about Knowledge, that of the scholar, the scientist, or anyone else: it always wants to blame the mind of the Uncarved Block — what *it* calls Ignorance — for problems that it causes itself, either directly or indirectly, through its own limitations, nearsightedness, or neglect. For example, if you build your house where the wind can blow it over, then let it go to pieces while you worry about how to spell *Marmalade*, what is likely to happen? Of course. Anyone knows that. Yet when Owl's house falls down, what does he have to say about it?

"Pooh," said Owl severely, "did *you* do that?"

"No," said Pooh humbly. "I don't *think* so."

"Then who did?"

"I think it was the wind," said Piglet. "I think your house has blown down."

"Oh, is that it? I thought it was Pooh."

"No," said Pooh.

For the chapter's concluding word about Knowledge for the sake of Knowledge, let's recall an incident from *The House at Pooh Corner*. Eeyore was busy intimidating Piglet with something he'd made from three sticks . . .

"Do you know what A means, little Piglet?"

"No, Eeyore, I don't."

"It means Learning, it means Education, it means all the things that you and Pooh haven't got. That's what A means."

"Oh," said Piglet again. "I mean, does it?" he explained quickly.

"I'm telling you. People come and go in this Forest, and they say, 'It's only Eeyore, so it doesn't count.' They walk to and fro saying 'Ha ha!' But do they know anything about A? They don't. It's just three sticks to *them*. But to the Educated – mark this, little Piglet – to the Educated, not meaning Poohs and Piglets, it's a great and glorious A. Not," he added, "just something that anybody can come and *breathe* on."

Then Rabbit came along . . .

"There's just one thing I wanted to ask you, Eeyore. What happens to Christopher Robin in the mornings nowadays?"

"What's this that I'm looking at?" said Eeyore, still looking at it.

"Three sticks," said Rabbit promptly.

"You see?" said Eeyore to Piglet. He turned to Rabbit. "I will now answer your question," he said solemnly.

"Thank you," said Rabbit.

"What does Christopher Robin do in the mornings? He learns. He becomes Educated. He instigorates — I *think* that is the word he mentioned, but I may be referring to something else — he instigorates Knowledge. In my small way I also, if I have the word right, am — am doing what he does. That, for instance, is — "

"An A," said Rabbit, "but not a very good one. Well, I must get back and tell the others."

Eeyore looked at his sticks and then he looked at Piglet . . .

"He *knew?* You mean this A thing is a thing *Rabbit* knew?"

"Yes, Eeyore. He's clever, Rabbit is."

"Clever!" said Eeyore scornfully, putting a foot heavily on his three sticks. "Education!" said Eeyore bitterly, jumping on his six sticks. "What *is* Learning?" asked Eeyore as he kicked his twelve sticks into the air. "A thing *Rabbit* knows! Ha!"

So there.

"I know something that Rabbit doesn't know," said Piglet.

"Oh? What's that?" I asked.

"Well, I can't remember what it's called, but – "

"Oh, yes. That's what's coming up next," I said.

"Oh, what *is* it called?" said Piglet, tapping his foot.

"Well, let's see . . ."

Cottleston Pie

Remember when Kanga and Roo came to the Forest? Immediately, Rabbit decided that he didn't like them, because they were Different. Then he began thinking of a way to make them leave. Fortunately for everyone, the plan failed, as Clever Plans do, sooner or later.

Cleverness, after all, has its limitations. Its mechanical judgments and clever remarks tend to prove inaccurate with passing time, because it doesn't look very deeply into things to begin with. As in Rabbit's case, it has to change its opinions later on because of what it didn't see when it was forming them. The thing that makes someone *truly* different — unique, in fact — is something that Cleverness cannot really understand.

We will refer to that special Something here as

Inner Nature. Since it's pretty much beyond the power of the intellect to measure or understand, we will have *Pooh* explain it to us, which he will do by way of the Cottleston Pie Principle.

"Er . . . (cough) . . . *Ahum*."

Excuse me a moment.

"Yes, Pooh?"
"*Me* explain it?" said Pooh behind his paw.
"Well, yes – I thought that might be nice."
"Why don't *you* explain it?" asked Pooh.
"Well, I thought it would be better if *you* did, somehow."
"I don't think that's such a good idea," said Pooh.
"Why not?"
"Because when I explain things, they get in the wrong places," he said. "That's why."
"All right, I'll explain it. But you can help out every now and then. How does that sound?"
"Much more like it," said Pooh.

Let's see. The Cottleston Pie Principle is based upon the song *Cottleston Pie*, which Pooh sang in *Winnie-the-Pooh*. Hmm . . .

"I say, Pooh. Maybe you'd better sing it again, in case anyone's forgotten."

"Certainly," said Pooh. "Now, let me see . . . (*ahem*),"

> *Cottleston, Cottleston, Cottleston Pie,*
> *A fly can't bird, but a bird can fly.*
> *Ask me a riddle and I reply:*
> *"<u>Cottleston, Cottleston, Cottleston Pie</u>."*

> *Cottleston, Cottleston, Cottleston Pie,*
> *A fish can't whistle and neither can I.*
> *Ask me a riddle and I reply:*
> *"Cottleston, <u>Cottleston, Cottleston Pie</u>."*

> *Cottleston, Cottleston, Cottleston Pie,*
> *Why does a chicken, I don't know why.*
> *Ask me a riddle and I reply:*
> *"<u>Cottleston, Cottleston, Cottleston Pie</u>."*

Now, let's start with – Ow! Oh, yes. "That was very nice, Pooh."

"Don't mention it."

Let's start with the first part: "A fly can't bird, but a bird can fly." Very simple. It's obvious, isn't it? And yet, you'd be surprised how many people violate this simple principle every day of their lives and try to fit square pegs into round holes, ignoring the clear reality that Things Are As They Are. We will let a selection from the writings of Chuang-tse illustrate:

> Hui-tse said to Chuang-tse, "I have a large tree which no carpenter can cut into lumber. Its branches and trunk are crooked and tough, covered with bumps and depressions. No builder would turn his head to look at it. Your teachings are the same – useless, without value. Therefore, no one pays attention to them."

> "As you know," Chuang-tse replied, "a cat is very skilled at capturing its prey. Crouching low, it can leap in any direction, pursuing whatever it is after. But when its attention is focused on such things, it can be easily caught with a net. On the other hand, a huge yak is not easily caught or overcome. It stands like a stone, or a cloud in the sky. But for all its strength, it cannot catch a mouse.

> "You complain that your tree is not valuable as lumber. But you could make use of the shade it provides, rest under its sheltering branches, and stroll beneath it, admiring its character and appearance. Since it would not be endangered by an axe, what could threaten its existence? It is useless to you only because you want to

make it into something else and do not use it in
its proper way."

In other words, everything has its own place and
function. That applies to people, although many don't
seem to realize it, stuck as they are in the wrong job,
the wrong marriage, or the wrong house. When you
know and respect your own Inner Nature, you know
where you belong. You also know where you *don't*
belong. One man's food is often another man's poison,
and what is glamorous and exciting to some can be a
dangerous trap to others. An incident in the life of
Chuang-tse can serve as an example:

> While sitting on the banks of the P'u River,
> Chuang-tse was approached by two representa-
> tives of the Prince of Ch'u, who offered him a
> position at court. Chuang-tse watched the water
> flowing by as if he had not heard. Finally, he
> remarked, "I am told that the Prince has a sacred
> tortoise, over two thousand years old, which is
> kept in a box, wrapped in silk and brocade." "That
> is true," the officials replied. "If the tortoise had
> been given a choice," Chuang-tse continued,
> "which do you think he would have liked better
> – to have been alive in the mud, or dead within
> the palace?" "To have been alive in the mud, of
> course," the men answered. "I too prefer the mud,"
> said Chuang-tse. "Good-bye."

"I like mud, too," said Pooh.

"Yes . . . well, anyway — "

"On a hot summer day? Nothing like it," he said.

"But the point is — "

"It keeps you cool," he said.

"That's not important here, Pooh," I said.

"It's *not?*" he asked in a shocked sort of way.

"I mean, there are other things to be — "

"How do you know?" said Pooh. "Have you ever tried it?"

"No, but — "

"Just the thing for a hot summer day," he continued, leaning back and closing his eyes. "Down by the river, covered with mud . . ."

"Look, Pooh — "

"Mud's nice," said Piglet, walking over to the writing table and looking up at us. "It adds color to your skin."

"Can't say *I* ever cared for it," said Owl, flying over and perching on the lamp. "It sticks in one's feathers. Rather disagreeable."

"You see?" I said. "Everyone's different. That's what we were discussing."

"I thought we were talking about mud," said Piglet.

"So did I," said Pooh.

"Well, I must get back to my encyclopedia," said Owl.

And now, if we can, let's go on to the second part: "A fish can't whistle and neither can I." Coming from a wise mind, such a statement would mean, "I have certain limitations, and I know what they are." Such a mind would act accordingly. There's nothing wrong with not being able to whistle, especially if you're a fish. But there can be lots of things wrong with blindly trying to do what you aren't designed for. Fish don't live in trees, and birds don't spend too much time underwater if they can help it. Unfortunately, some *people* — who always seem to think they're smarter than fish and birds, somehow — aren't so wise, and end up causing big trouble for themselves and others.

That doesn't mean that we need to stop changing and improving. It just means that we need to recognize What's There. If you face the fact that you have weak muscles, say, then you can do the right things and eventually become strong. But if you ignore What's There and try to lift someone's car out of a ditch, what sort of condition will you be in after a while? And even if you have more muscle than anyone alive, you still can't push over a freight train. The wise know their limitations; the foolish do not.

To demonstrate what we mean, we can think of no one better than Tigger, who doesn't know his limitations.

Oh, excuse me. He says he does *now*.

Well, let's recall how he was forced to recognize *one* of them, anyway. Roo and Tigger were walking through the Forest one morning, and Tigger was talking about all the things that Tiggers can do . . .

> "Can they fly?" asked Roo.
>
> "Yes," said Tigger, "they're very good flyers, Tiggers are, Stornry good flyers."
>
> "Oo!" said Roo. "Can they fly as well as Owl?"
>
> "Yes," said Tigger. "Only they don't want to."

Well, after this sort of talk had gone on for a while, they arrived at the Six Pine Trees:

> "I can swim," said Roo. "I fell into the river, and I swimmed. Can Tiggers swim?"
>
> "Of course they can. Tiggers can do everything."
>
> "Can they climb trees better than Pooh?" asked Roo, stopping under the tallest Pine Tree, and looking up at it.
>
> "Climbing trees is what they do best," said Tigger. "Much better than Poohs."

And the next thing they knew, they were stuck in the tallest pine tree. Well, well. Not so good.

But then Pooh and Piglet came along, and of course Pooh realized right away just what was happening. Well, not *right* away . . .

"It's a Jagular," he said.

"What do Jagulars do?" asked Piglet, hoping that they wouldn't.

"They hide in the branches of trees, and drop on you as you go underneath," said Pooh. "Christopher Robin told me."

"Perhaps we better hadn't go underneath, Pooh. In case he dropped and hurt himself."

"They don't hurt themselves," said Pooh. "They're such very good droppers."

Piglet still felt that to be underneath a Very Good Dropper would be a Mistake, and he was just going to hurry back for something which he had forgotten when the Jagular called out to them.

"Help! Help!" it called.

"That's what Jagulars always do," said Pooh, much interested. "They call 'Help! Help!' and then when you look up, they drop on you."

But eventually, Christopher Robin and Eeyore came along, and a Rescue Net was formed. Then Roo jumped and was Saved, and Tigger jumped (sort of) . . .
. . . and was Saved (sort of):

There was a crash, and a tearing noise, and a confused heap of everybody on the ground.

Christopher Robin and Pooh and Piglet picked themselves up first, and then they picked Tigger up, and underneath everybody else was Eeyore.

"Quite a bit of trouble you put everyone through, wasn't it, Tigger?"
"I learned from the experience, though," he said, a bit evasively.
"Oh, did you?"

"Of course. You won't find me doing anything like *that* again," he said in a confident sort of way.

"That's good," I said. "On your way to somewhere, are you?"

"Yes," he said. "Roo and I are going swimming."

"Oh. Well, don't forget to take a rope."

"A rope? Why a rope?" said Tigger.

"Oh, just in case you see somebody fall in," I said.

"Now why didn't *I* think of that?" said Tigger.

A saying from the area of Chinese medicine would be appropriate to mention here: "One disease, long life; no disease, short life." In other words, those who know what's wrong with them and take care of themselves accordingly will tend to live a lot longer than those who consider themselves perfectly healthy and neglect their weaknesses. So, in that sense at least, a Weakness of some sort can do you a big favor, *if* you acknowledge that it's there. The same goes for one's limitations, whether Tiggers know it or not – and Tiggers usually don't. That's the trouble with Tiggers, you know: they can do *everything*. Very unhealthy.

Once you face and understand your limitations, you can work *with* them, instead of having them work against you and get in your way, which is what they do when you ignore them, whether you realize it or not. And then you will find that, in many cases, your limitations can be your strengths.

For example, when Owl's house fell down, who was able to escape, even though there was a heavy branch across the door and the only way out was through the letter-box?

Piglet, the Very Small Animal.

Now, the last part of the principle: "Why does a chicken, I don't know why." Why does a chicken do what it does? You don't know? Neither do we. Neither does anyone else. Science likes to strut around and Act Smart by putting its labels on everything, but if you look at them closely, you'll see that they don't really say much. "Genes"? "DNA"? Just scratching the surface. "Instinct"? You know what *that* means:

> CURIOUS: "Why do birds fly South for the winter?"
> SCIENCE. "Instinct."

It means, "We don't know."

The important thing is, we don't really *need* to know. We don't need to imitate Nearsighted Science, which peers at the world through an electron microscope, looking for answers it will never find and coming up with more questions instead. We don't need to play Abstract Philosopher, asking unnecessary questions and coming up with meaningless answers. What we need to do is recognize Inner Nature and work with Things As They Are. When we don't, we get into trouble.

Pooh and Piglet found this out when they tried to catch a Heffalump. Not really knowing what Heffalumps like to eat, Piglet assumed that they would be attracted by acorns, and Pooh thought – but first, you remember what a Heffalump is, don't you?

> One day, when Christopher Robin and Winnie-the-Pooh and Piglet were all talking together, Christopher Robin finished the mouthful he was eating and said carelessly: "I saw a Heffalump today, Piglet."
>
> "What was it doing?" asked Piglet.
>
> "Just lumping along," said Christopher Robin. "I don't think it saw *me*."
>
> "I saw one once," said Piglet. "At least, I think I did," he said. "Only perhaps it wasn't."
>
> "So did I," said Pooh, wondering what a Heffalump was like.
>
> "You don't often see them," said Christopher Robin carelessly.
>
> "Not now," said Piglet.
>
> "Not at this time of year," said Pooh.

That's what a Heffalump is. So Pooh and Piglet decided to capture one. The plan started out well . . .

> Pooh's first idea was that they should dig a Very Deep Pit, and then the Heffalump would come along and fall into the Pit, and –

"Why?" said Piglet.

"Why what?" said Pooh.

"Why would he fall in?"

Pooh rubbed his nose with his paw, and said that the Heffalump might be walking along, humming a little song, and looking up at the sky, wondering if it would rain, and so he wouldn't see the Very Deep Pit until he was half-way down, when it would be too late.

Piglet said that this was a very good Trap, but supposing it were raining already?

Pooh rubbed his nose again, and said that he hadn't thought of that. And then he brightened up, and said that, if it were raining already, the Heffalump would be looking at the sky wondering if it would *clear up*, and so he wouldn't see the Very Deep Pit until he was half-way down.... When it would be too late.

Piglet said that, now that this point had been explained, he thought it was a Cunning Trap.

Pooh was very proud when he heard this, and he felt that the Heffalump was as good as caught already, but there was just one other thing which had to be thought about, and it was this. *Where should they dig the Very Deep Pit?*

Piglet said that the best place would be somewhere where a Heffalump was, just before he fell into it, only about a foot farther on.

"But then he would see us digging it," said Pooh.

"Not if he was looking at the sky."

It sounds easy, doesn't it? Let's see. First, you dig a hole . . .

. . . making sure that it's big enough for a Heffalump.

And the best way to make sure that the Heffalump gets into the Trap once you've made it is to put something that Heffalumps like into it, such as a bag of peanuts, or –

"Honey," said Pooh.

"*Honey?*"

"A jar of honey," said Pooh.

"Are you sure?"

"A big jar of honey," Pooh insisted.

"Who ever heard of Heffalumps liking *honey?* Sticky, gooey . . . How would they ever – "

"The best thing," said Pooh.

All right, *honey.* You put the honey in the Trap, and before you know it, you've caught a . . .

Hmm. Something went wrong. That's not a Heffalump. But what is it? Maybe Piglet will find out when he goes to see what's in the Trap.

"Help, help!" cried Piglet, "a Heffalump, a Horrible Heffalump!" and he scampered off as hard as he could, still crying out, "Help, help, a Herrible Hoffalump! Hoff, Hoff, a Hellible Horralump! Holl, Holl, a Hoffable Hellerump!" And he didn't stop crying and scampering until he got to Christopher Robin's house.

"Whatever's the matter, Piglet?" said Christopher Robin who was just getting up.

"Heff," said Piglet, breathing so hard that he could hardly speak, "a Hell – a Heff – a Heffalump."

"Where?"

"Up there," said Piglet, waving his paw.

"What did it look like?"

"Like – like – It had the biggest head you ever saw, Christopher Robin. A great enormous thing, like – like nothing. A huge big – well, like a – I don't know – like an enormous big nothing. Like a jar."

So the honey wasn't such a good thing to use, after all. We didn't think that it really matched the Nature of Heffalumps, somehow.

Now that we know the principle, we can – "Oh, it's you, Pooh."

"Mufflewuffle *Cottleston Pie* mufflewuffle."

"I beg your pardon?"

"Tell them about *Cottleston Pie* – what it means," Pooh whispered, a little more clearly.

"I just did," I said.

"I mean, tell them what it *stands* for," said Pooh expectantly.

"Oh, of course. Thank you, Pooh."

Pooh wants us to know that the words *Cottleston Pie* are a way of saying *Inner Nature*. So, by substituting that term for the last line in each verse of the song, we get:

Ask me a riddle and I reply:
<u>*"Inner Nature."*</u>

Hmm.

"*Cottleston Pie* sounds better," said Pooh.

"Well, how about this, Pooh?"

Ask me a riddle and I reply:
"Things Are As They Are."

"Better . . . But it still doesn't rhyme."
"All right, how's *this?*"

Ask me a riddle and I reply:
"Cottleston, Cottleston, Cottleston Pie."

"Just right," said Pooh.

Now that we know the principle, we can look at its applications. As we have likely recognized by now, no two snowflakes, trees, or animals are alike. No two *people* are the same, either. Everything has its own Inner Nature. Unlike other forms of life, though, people are easily led away from what's right for them, because people have Brain, and Brain can be fooled. Inner Nature, when relied on, cannot be fooled. But many people do not look at it or listen to it, and consequently do not understand themselves very much. Having little understanding of themselves, they have little respect for themselves, and are therefore easily influenced by others.

But, rather than be carried along by circumstances and manipulated by those who can see the weaknesses and behavior tendencies that we ignore, we can work with our own characteristics and be in control of our own lives. The Way of Self-Reliance starts with recognizing who we are, what we've got to work with, and what works best for us.

"How would *you* explain it, Pooh?"

"With a song," he said. "A little something I just made up."

"Go ahead."

"Certainly . . . (cough)."

How can you get very far,
If you don't know Who You Are?
How can you do what you ought,
If you don't know What You've Got?
And if you don't know Which To Do
Of all the things in front of you,
Then what you'll have when you are through
Is just a mess without a clue
Of all the best that can come true
If you know What and Which and Who.

"That's it," he said, leaning back and closing his eyes.

"A Masterpiece."

"Well, better than average, maybe."

Sooner or later, we are bound to discover some things about ourselves that we don't like. But once we see they're there, we can decide what we want to do with them. Do we want to get rid of them completely, change them into other things, or use them in beneficial ways? The last two approaches are often especially Useful, since they avoid head-on conflict, and therefore minimize struggle. Also, they allow those transformed characteristics to be added to the list of things we have that help us out.

In a similar manner, instead of struggling to erase what are referred to as negative emotions, we can learn to use them in positive ways. We could describe the principle like this: while pounding on the piano keys may produce noise, removing them doesn't exactly further the creation of music. The principles of Music and Living aren't all that different, we think.

"Wouldn't you say, Pooh?"
"Say what?" asked Pooh, opening his eyes.
"Music and Living — "
"The same thing," said Pooh.

That's what we thought. So rather than work against ourselves, all we need to do in many cases is to point our weaknesses or unpleasant tendencies in a different direction than we have been.

The following incident recorded by the Taoist Liu An can serve to illustrate:

In the state of Ch'u, a housebreaker became a soldier under the General Tzu-fa, a man known for utilizing the abilities of others to a remarkable degree.

A short while later, Ch'u was attacked by the army of the state of Ch'i. Tzu-fa's men went out to counter the attack, but were driven back three times. The Ch'u strategists exhausted their minds while the enemy forces grew stronger.

At that point, the housebreaker stepped forward and asked for a chance to work for the defense of Ch'u. The General granted his request.

That night, the housebreaker sneaked into the Ch'i camp, entered the general's tent, and removed the curtains from the bed. Tzu-fa sent these back the next morning by special envoy, with a note which explained that they had been found by some men who were out gathering firewood.

The following evening, the housebreaker removed the Ch'i general's pillow. The next morning, it was returned with a message like the first.

On the third night, the housebreaker removed the general's jade hairpin. It was returned the next morning.

That day, the Ch'i general called his officers together. "One more night," he warned them, "and it will be my *head*!" The troops were ordered to break camp and return home.

So there is no such thing as an ability that is too useless, too crooked, or too small. It only depends on what you do with it. As Lao-tse pointed out, the bad can be raw material for the good.

So quite often, the easiest way to get rid of a Minus is to change it into a Plus. Sometimes you will find that characteristics you try hard to eliminate eventually come back, anyway. But if you do the right things, they will come back in the right ways. And sometimes those very tendencies that you dislike the most can show up in the right way at the right time to save your life, somehow. If that's ever happened to you, you'll think twice before setting out to completely Unbounce yourself.

What do we mean by Unbounce yourself? Well, you remember the situation with Tigger . . .

"How did you fall in, Eeyore?" asked Rabbit, as he dried him with Piglet's handkerchief.

"I didn't," said Eeyore.

"But how — "

"I was BOUNCED," said Eeyore.

"Oo," said Roo excitedly, "did somebody push you?"

"Somebody BOUNCED me. I was just thinking by the side of the river – thinking, if any of you know what that means, when I received a loud BOUNCE."

"Oh, Eeyore!" said everybody.

"Are you sure you didn't slip?" asked Rabbit wisely.

"Of course I slipped. If you're standing on the slippery bank of a river, and somebody BOUNCES you loudly from behind, you slip. What did you think I did?"

"But who did it?" asked Roo.

Eeyore didn't answer.

"I expect it was Tigger," said Piglet nervously.

"But, Eeyore," said Pooh, "was it a Joke, or an Accident? I mean – "

"I didn't stop to ask, Pooh. Even at the very bottom of the river I didn't stop to say to myself, '*Is* this a Hearty Joke, or is it the Merest Accident?' I just floated to the surface, and said to myself, 'It's wet.' If you know what I mean."

So, to remove the Bounce from Tigger, Rabbit came up with another one of his famous plans: Rabbit, Pooh, and Piglet would take Tigger to somewhere at the top of the Forest where he'd never been, and lose him there. And from then on, he would be a Small and Sorry Tigger who bounced no more. Well, so much for Cleverness, as Eeyore might say, because as things turned out, Rabbit got *everyone* lost, including himself. Everyone but Tigger, that is. Tiggers don't get lost, it so happens, not even in the mist at the top of the Forest. And that proved to be very Useful.

Because, although Pooh and Piglet found their way back after a while . . .

"Where's Rabbit?"

"I don't know," said Pooh.

"Oh — well, I expect Tigger will find him. He's sort of looking for you all."

"Well," said Pooh, "I've got to go home for something, and so has Piglet, because we haven't had it yet, and — "

"I'll come and watch you," said Christopher Robin.

So he went home with Pooh, and watched him for quite a long time . . . and all the time he was watching, Tigger was tearing round the Forest making loud yapping noises for Rabbit. And at last a very Small and Sorry Rabbit heard him. And the Small and Sorry Rabbit rushed through the mist at the noise, and it suddenly turned into Tigger; a Friendly Tigger, a Grand Tigger, a Large and Helpful Tigger, a Tigger who bounced, if he bounced at all, in just the beautiful way a Tigger ought to bounce.

"Oh, Tigger, I *am* glad to see you," cried Rabbit.

In the story of the Ugly Duckling, when did the Ugly Duckling stop feeling Ugly? When he realized that he was a Swan. Each of us has something Special, a Swan of some sort, hidden inside somewhere. But until we recognize that it's there, what can we do but splash around, treading water? The Wise are Who They Are. They work with what they've got and do what they can do.

There are things about ourselves that we need to get rid of; there are things we need to change. But at the same time, we do not need to be too desperate, too ruthless, too combative. Along the way to usefulness and happiness, many of those things will change themselves, and the others can be worked on as we go. The first thing we need to do is recognize and trust our own Inner Nature, and not lose sight of it. For within the Ugly Duckling is the Swan, inside the Bouncy Tigger is the Rescuer who knows the Way, and in each of us is something Special, and that we need to keep.

> For a long time they looked at the river beneath them, saying nothing, and the river said nothing too, for it felt very quiet and peaceful on this summer afternoon.
>
> "Tigger is all right *really*," said Piglet lazily.
>
> "Of course he is," said Christopher Robin.
>
> "Everybody is *really*," said Pooh. "That's what *I* think," said Pooh. "But I don't suppose I'm right," he said.
>
> "Of course you are," said Christopher Robin.

The Pooh Way

By the time it came to the edge of the Forest the stream had grown-up, so that it was almost a river, and, being grown-up, it did not run and jump and sparkle along as it used to do when it was younger, but moved more slowly. For it knew now where it was going, and it said to itself, "There is no hurry. We shall get there some day."

Now we come to what could be called the most characteristic element of Taoism-in-action. In Chinese, it is known as *Wu Wei*. It is also the most characteristic element of Pooh-in-action. In English, it is not known as much of anything in particular. We believe that it's time that someone noticed it and called it something, so we will call it the Pooh Way.

Literally, *Wu Wei* means "without doing, causing,

or making." But practically speaking, it means without meddlesome, combative, or egotistical effort. It seems rather significant that the character *Wei* developed from the symbols for a clawing hand and a monkey, since the term *Wu Wei* means no going against the nature of things; no clever tampering; no Monkeying Around.

The efficiency of *Wu Wei* is like that of water flowing over and around the rocks in its path – not the mechanical, straight-line approach that usually ends up short-circuiting natural laws, but one that evolves from an inner sensitivity to the natural rhythm of things.

Let's take an example from the writings of Chuang-tse:

> At the Gorge of Lü, the great waterfall plunges for thousands of feet, its spray visible for miles. In the churning waters below, no living creature can be seen.

> One day, K'ung Fu-tse was standing at a distance from the pool's edge, when he saw an old man being tossed about in the turbulent water. He called to his disciples, and together they ran to rescue the victim. But by the time they reached the water, the old man had climbed out onto the bank and was walking along, singing to himself.

K'ung Fu-tse hurried up to him. "You would have to be a ghost to survive that," he said, "but you seem to be a man, instead. What secret power do you have?"

"Nothing special," the old man replied. "I began to learn while very young, and grew up practicing it. Now I am certain of success. I go down with the water and come up with the water. I follow it and forget myself. I survive because I don't struggle against the water's superior power. That's all."

When we learn to work with our own Inner Nature, and with the natural laws operating around us, we reach the level of *Wu Wei*. Then we work with the natural order of things and operate on the principle of minimal effort. Since the natural world follows that principle, it does not make mistakes. Mistakes are made – or imagined – by man, the creature with the overloaded Brain who separates himself from the supporting network of natural laws by interfering and trying too hard.

Not like Pooh, the most *effortless* Bear we've ever seen.

"Just how do you do it, Pooh?"
"Do what?" asked Pooh.
"Become so Effortless."

"I don't *do* much of anything," he said.

"But all those things of yours get done."

"They just sort of happen," he said.

"Wait a minute. That reminds me of something from the *Tao Tê Ching*," I said, reaching for a book. "Here it is – chapter thirty-seven. Translated, it reads something like, 'Tao does not do, but nothing is not done.' "

"That sounds like a Riddle," said Pooh.

"It means that Tao doesn't force or interfere with things, but lets them work in their own way, to produce results naturally. Then whatever needs to be done is done."

"I see," said Pooh.

"In Chinese, the principle would be *Wei Wu Wei* – 'Do Without Doing.' From *Wei Wu Wei* comes *Tzu Jan*, 'Self So.' That means that things happen by themselves, spontaneously."

"Oh, I see," said Pooh.

For a basic example of the Pooh Way, let's recall something that happened in *The House at Pooh Corner* when Pooh, Piglet, Rabbit, and Roo were playing Poohsticks. They'd dropped their sticks off the bridge into the river, and had gone to the other side to see whose stick would come out first.

And they'd been waiting quite a while when out floated . . .

Eeyore. *Eeyore?*

"I didn't know you were playing," said Roo.

"I'm not," said Eeyore.

"Eeyore, what *are* you doing there?" said Rabbit.

"I'll give you three guesses, Rabbit. Digging holes in the ground? Wrong. Leaping from branch to branch of a young oak-tree? Wrong. Waiting for somebody to help me out of the river? Right. Give Rabbit time, and he'll always get the answer."

Then Pooh got an idea. They could drop some stones into the river, the stones would make waves, and the waves would wash Eeyore over to the river bank. Rabbit thought it was a good idea. Eeyore didn't.

"Supposing we hit him by mistake?" said Piglet anxiously.

"Or supposing you missed him by mistake," said Eeyore. "Think of all the possibilities, Piglet, before you settle down to enjoy yourselves."

But Pooh had got the biggest stone he could carry, and was leaning over the bridge, holding it in his paws.

"I'm not throwing it, I'm dropping it, Eeyore,"

he explained. "And then I can't miss – I mean I can't hit you. *Could* you stop turning round for a moment, because it muddles me rather?"

"No," said Eeyore. "I *like* turning round."

Rabbit began to feel that it was time he took command.

"Now, Pooh," he said, "when I say 'Now!' you can drop it. Eeyore, when I say 'Now!' Pooh will drop his stone."

"Thank you very much, Rabbit, but I expect I shall know."

"Are you ready, Pooh? Piglet, give Pooh a little more room. Get back a bit there, Roo. Are you ready?"

"No," said Eeyore.

"*Now!*" said Rabbit.

Pooh dropped his stone. There was a loud splash, and Eeyore disappeared. . . .

It was an anxious moment for the watchers on the bridge. They looked and looked . . . and even the sight of Piglet's stick coming out a little in front of Rabbit's didn't cheer them up as much as you would have expected. And then, just as Pooh was beginning to think that he must have chosen the wrong stone or the wrong river or the wrong day for his Idea, something grey showed for a moment by the river bank . . . and it got slowly bigger and bigger . . . and at last it was Eeyore coming out.

With a shout they rushed off the bridge, and pushed and pulled at him; and soon he was standing among them again on dry land.

"Oh, Eeyore, you *are* wet!" said Piglet, feeling him.

Eeyore shook himself, and asked somebody to explain to Piglet what happened when you had been inside a river for quite a long time.

"Well done, Pooh," said Rabbit kindly. "That was a good idea of ours."

Cleverness, as usual, takes all the credit it possibly can. But it's not the Clever Mind that's responsible when things work out. It's the mind that sees what's in front of it, and follows the nature of things.

When you work with *Wu Wei*, you put the round peg in the round hole and the square peg in the square hole. No stress, no struggle. Egotistical Desire tries to force the round peg into the square hole and the square peg into the round hole. Cleverness tries to devise craftier ways of making pegs fit where they don't belong. Knowledge tries to figure out why round pegs fit round holes, but not square holes. *Wu Wei* doesn't try. It doesn't think about it. It just does it. And when it does, it doesn't appear to do much of anything. But Things Get Done.

"Having trouble, Piglet?"

"The lid on this jar is *stuck*," gasped Piglet.

"Yes, it . . . *is*, isn't it. Here, Pooh, *you* open it." (Pop.)

"Thanks, Pooh," said Piglet.

"Nothing, really," said Pooh.

"How did you get that lid off?" asked Tigger.

"It's easy," said Pooh. "You just twist on it like this, until you can't twist any harder. Then you take a deep breath and, as you let it out, *twist*. That's all."

"Let me try that!" yelled Tigger, bouncing into the kitchen. "Where's that new jar of pickles? Ah, here it is."

"Tigger," began Piglet nervously, "I don't think you'd better – "

"Nothing to it," said Tigger. "Just twist, and – "

CRASH!

"All right, Tigger," I said. "Get those pickles off the floor."

"Slipped out of my paw," explained Tigger.

"He tried too hard," said Pooh.

And when you try too hard, it doesn't work. Try grabbing something quickly and precisely with a tensed-up arm; then relax and try it again. Try doing something with a tense mind. The surest way to become Tense, Awkward, and Confused is to develop a mind that tries too hard – one that thinks too much. The animals in the Forest don't think too much; they just Are. But with an overwhelming number of people, to misquote an old Western philosopher, it's a case of "I think, therefore I am Confused." If you compare the City with the Forest, you may begin to wonder why it's *man* who goes around classifying himself as The Superior Animal.

"Superior to what?" asked Pooh.

"I don't know, Pooh. I've tried to think of *something*, but I just can't come up with an answer."

"If people were Superior to Animals, they'd take better care of the world," said Pooh.

"That's true," I said.

But down through the centuries, man has developed a mind that separates him from the world of reality, the world of natural laws. This mind tries too hard, wears itself out, and ends up weak and sloppy. Such a mind, even if of high intelligence, is inefficient. It goes here and there, backwards and forwards, and fails to concentrate on what it's doing at the moment. It drives down the street in a fast-moving car and thinks it's at the store, going over a grocery list. Then it wonders why accidents occur.

When you work with *Wu Wei*, you have no real accidents. Things may get a little Odd at times, but they work out. You don't have to try very hard to *make* them work out; you just *let* them. For example, let's recall the Search for Small. Small – which is short for Very Small Beetle, we were told – disappeared one day on his way around a gorse-bush. Nobody knew what happened.

So the Search was begun, and soon everyone was trying very hard to find Small. Everyone, of course, had been organized and directed by Rabbit. Everyone, of course, except for Pooh:

Bump!

"Ow!" squeaked something.

"That's funny," thought Pooh. "I said 'Ow!' without really oo'ing."

"Help!" said a small, high voice.

"That's me again," thought Pooh. "I've had an Accident, and fallen down a well, and my voice has gone all squeaky and works before I'm ready for it, because I've done something to myself inside. Bother!"

"Help – help!"

"There you are! I say things when I'm not trying. So it must be a very bad Accident." And then he thought that perhaps when he did try to say things he wouldn't be able to; so, to make sure, he said loudly: "A Very Bad Accident to Pooh Bear."

"Pooh!" squeaked the voice.

"It's Piglet!" cried Pooh eagerly. "Where are you?"

"Underneath," said Piglet in an underneath sort of way.

"Underneath what?"

Well, after *that* had been straightened out . . .

"Pooh!" he cried. "There's something climbing up your back."

"I thought there was," said Pooh.

"It's Small!" cried Piglet.

Those who do things by the Pooh Way find this sort of thing happening to them all the time. It's hard to explain, except by example, but it works. Things just happen in the right way, at the right time. At least they do when you *let* them, when you work *with* circumstances instead of saying, "This isn't supposed to be happening this way," and trying hard to make it happen some other way. If you're in tune with The Way Things Work, then they work the way they need to, no matter what you may think about it at the time. Later on, you can look back and say, "Oh, now I understand. That had to happen so that *those* could happen, and those had to happen in order for *this* to happen. . ." Then you realize that even if you'd tried to make it all turn out perfectly, you couldn't have done better, and if you'd *really* tried, you would have made a mess of the whole thing.

Let's take another example of Things Work Out: Eeyore's birthday party, as arranged by Pooh and Piglet.

Pooh discovered, after Eeyore told him, that it was Eeyore's birthday. So Pooh decided to give him something. He went home to get a jar of honey to use as a birthday present, and talked things over with Piglet, who decided to give Eeyore a balloon that he'd saved from a party of his own. While Piglet went to get the balloon, Pooh walked off to Eeyore's with the jar of honey.

But after a while, he began to get Hungry.

> So he sat down and took the top off his jar of honey. "Lucky I brought this with me," he thought. "Many a bear going out on a warm day like this would never have thought of bringing a little something with him." And he began to eat.

> "Now let me see," he thought, as he took his last lick of the inside of the jar, "where was I going? Ah, yes, Eeyore." He got up slowly.

And then, suddenly, he remembered. He had eaten Eeyore's birthday present!

Well, most of it, anyway. Fortunately, he still had the *jar.* And since he was passing by the Hundred Acre Wood, he went in to see Owl and had him write "*A Happy Birthday*" on it. After all, it *was* a nice jar, even with nothing in it.

> While all this was happening, Piglet had gone back to his own house to get Eeyore's balloon. He held it very tightly against himself, so that it shouldn't blow away, and he ran as fast as he could so as to get to Eeyore before Pooh did; for he thought that he would like to be the first one to give a present, just as if he had thought of it without being told by anybody. And running along, and thinking how pleased Eeyore would be, he didn't look where he was going . . . and suddenly he put his foot in a rabbit hole, and fell down flat on his face.

BANG!!!???★★★!!!

Yes, well, after Piglet fell on Eeyore's balloon, it wasn't so . . . well, it was more . . . that is, it was . . .

"*Balloon?*" said Eeyore. "You did say balloon? One of those big coloured things you blow up? Gaiety, song-and-dance, here we are and there we are?"

"Yes, but I'm afraid – I'm very sorry, Eeyore – but when I was running along to bring it to you, I fell down."

"Dear, dear, how unlucky! You ran too fast, I expect. You didn't hurt yourself, Little Piglet?"

"No, but I – I – oh, Eeyore, I burst the balloon!"

There was a very long silence.

"My balloon?" said Eeyore at last.

Piglet nodded.

"My birthday balloon?"

"Yes, Eeyore," said Piglet sniffing a little. "Here it is. With – with many happy returns of the day." And he gave Eeyore the small piece of damp rag.

"Is this it?" said Eeyore, a little surprised.

Piglet nodded.

"My present?"

Piglet nodded again.

"The balloon?"

And just then, Pooh arrived.

"I've brought you a little present," said Pooh excitedly.

"I've had it," said Eeyore.

Pooh had now splashed across the stream to Eeyore, and Piglet was sitting a little way off, his head in his paws, snuffling to himself.

"It's a Useful Pot," said Pooh. "Here it is. And it's got 'A Very Happy Birthday with love from Pooh' written on it. That's what all that writing is. And it's for putting things in. There!"

Then Eeyore discovered that, since the balloon was no longer as big as Piglet, it could easily be put away in the Useful Pot and taken out whenever it was needed, which certainly can't be done with the typical Unmanageable Balloon . . .

> "I'm very glad," said Pooh happily, "that I thought of giving you a Useful Pot to put things in."
>
> "I'm very glad," said Piglet happily, "that I thought of giving you Something to put in a Useful Pot."
>
> But Eeyore wasn't listening. He was taking the balloon out, and putting it back again, as happy as could be. . . .

So it all worked out.

At its highest level, *Wu Wei* is indefinable and practically invisible, because it has become a reflex action. In the words of Chuang-tse, the mind of *Wu Wei* "flows like water, reflects like a mirror, and responds like an echo."

Just like Pooh. "*Ahem.* I say, '*Just like Pooh.*' "

"Wh — what?" said Pooh, waking up suddenly and falling out of the chair. "What's like who?"

"What flows like water, reflects like a mirror, and responds like an echo?"

"Oh, a Riddle," said Pooh. "How many guesses do I get?"

"Oh, I don't know. Let's just see what happens."

"What could it be?" he mumbled. "Flows like water . . ."

Using *Wu Wei*, you go by circumstances and listen to your own intuition. "This isn't the best time to do this. I'd better go *that* way." Like that. When you do that sort of thing, people may say you have a Sixth Sense or something. All it really is, though, is being Sensitive to Circumstances. That's just natural. It's only strange when you *don't* listen.

One of the most convenient things about this Sensitivity to Circumstances is that you don't have to make so many difficult decisions. Instead, you can let them make themselves.

For example, in *The House at Pooh Corner*, Pooh was wandering around one day trying to decide whom he wanted to visit. He could go see Eeyore, whom he hadn't seen since yesterday, or Owl, whom he hadn't seen since the day before yesterday, or Kanga, Roo, and Tigger, all of whom he hadn't seen for quite a while. How did he decide? He sat down on a rock in the middle of the stream and sang a song.

Then he got up and wandered around again, thinking about visiting Rabbit, until he found himself at his own front door. He went inside, got something to eat, and then went out to see Piglet.

That's how it is when you use the Pooh Way. Nothing to it. No stress, no mess. Now —

"A stream?" asked Pooh.

"What?"

"The answer. A *stream* flows like water, reflects like a mirror — "

"But it doesn't respond like an echo," I said.

"Yes, it does," said Pooh.

"Well, you're *close*. Sort of. I guess."

"Just give me more time," said Pooh.

The *Wu Wei* approach to conflict-solving can be seen in the practice of the Taoist martial art *T'ai Chi Ch'üan*, the basic idea of which is to wear the opponent out either by sending his energy back at him or by deflecting it away, in order to weaken his power, balance, and position-for-defense. Never is force opposed with force; instead, it is overcome with yielding.

"Flows like water, reflects like a mirror . . .," said Pooh, walking by.

"You're thinking too much, Pooh," I said. "I'll give you a hint; maybe it'll help."

"I hope so," said Pooh. "This is beginning to Bother me."

"All right — to solve the Riddle, you need to let your mind *flow* along and *reflect* what it sees. Then it can *respond* with the answer. Get it?"

"No," said Pooh.

"Oh, well."

"Let me see — flows like water . . .," muttered Pooh.

The *Wu Wei* principle underlying *T'ai Chi Ch'üan* can be understood by striking at a piece of cork floating in water. The harder you hit it, the more it yields; the more it yields, the harder it bounces back. Without expending energy, the cork can easily wear you out. So, *Wu Wei* overcomes force by neutralizing its power, rather than by adding to the conflict. With other approaches, you may fight fire with fire, but with *Wu Wei*, you fight fire with water.

"*I* know," said Pooh. "A piece of cork!"

"What about it?"

"Responds like an echo!" he said triumphantly.

"But it doesn't flow like water or reflect like a mirror," I said.

"Oh," said Pooh. "That's right."

"Well, I guess I'd better tell you," I said. "It's the Pooh Way."

"What is?" asked Pooh.

"The answer," I said.

"Oh," said Pooh.

"That wasn't a very good Riddle," he added.

"All right, then *you* ask one."

"Glad to. What's black and white and red all over?"

"Oh, no. Not *that* one."

"You've heard it before?" asked Pooh, a bit surprised.

"Of course. It's been around for years. Everyone knows the answer – It's a newspaper."

"No," said Pooh.

"An embarrassed zebra?"

"No."

"Well, then . . ."

"Give up?" Pooh asked hopefully.

"All right, I give up. What's black and white and red all over?"

"A sunburned penguin."

"Pooh, that's stupid."

"Better than yours," he said.

"Well, here's another one, then. It has to do with the opposite of the Pooh Way. What runs around all day without getting anywhere?"

"A Rabbit?" said Pooh.

"Well, *practically*."

"Oh, I know. It's a — "

But we're saving *that* for the next chapter.

Bisy Backson

Rabbit hurried on by the edge of the Hundred Acre Wood, feeling more important every minute, and soon he came to the tree where Christopher Robin lived. He knocked at the door, and he called out once or twice, and then he walked back a little way and put his paw up to keep the sun out, and called to the top of the tree, and then he turned all round and shouted "Hallo!" and "I say!" "It's Rabbit!" – but nothing happened. Then he stopped and listened, and everything stopped and listened with him, and the Forest was very lone and still and peaceful in the sunshine, until suddenly a hundred miles above him a lark began to sing.

"Bother!" said Rabbit. "He's gone out."

He went back to the green front door, just to

make sure, and he was turning away, feeling that his morning had got all spoilt, when he saw a piece of paper on the ground. And there was a pin in it, as if it had fallen off the door.

"Ha!" said Rabbit, feeling quite happy again. "Another notice!"

This is what it said:

GON OUT

BACKSON

BISY

BACKSON.

C. R.

Rabbit didn't know what a Backson was — in spite of the fact that he is one — so he went to ask Owl. Owl didn't know, either. But we think *we* know, and we think a lot of other people do, too. Chuang-tse described one quite accurately:

There was a man who disliked seeing his footprints and his shadow. He decided to escape from them, and began to run. But as he ran along, more footprints appeared, while his shadow easily kept up with him. Thinking he was going too slowly, he ran faster and faster without stopping, until he finally collapsed from exhaustion and died.

If he had stood still, there would have been no footprints. If he had rested in the shade, his shadow would have disappeared.

You see them almost everywhere you go, it seems. On practically any sunny sort of day, you can see the Backsons stampeding through the park, making all kinds of loud Breathing Noises. Perhaps you are enjoying a picnic on the grass when you suddenly look up to find that one or two of them just ran over your lunch.

Generally, though, you are safe around trees and grass, as Backsons tend to avoid them. They prefer instead to struggle along on asphalt and concrete, in imitation of the short-lived transportation machines for which those hard surfaces were designed. Inhaling poisonous exhaust fumes from the vehicles that swerve to avoid hitting them, the Backsons blabber away to each other about how much better they feel now that they have gone Outdoors. Natural living, they call it.

The Bisy Backson is almost desperately active. If you ask him what his Life Interests are, he will give you a list of Physical Activities, such as:

"Skydiving, tennis, jogging, racquet-ball, skiing, swimming, and water-skiing."

"Is that all?"

"Well, I (gasp, pant, wheeze) *think* so," says Backson.

"Have you ever tried chasing cars?"

"No, I – no, I never have."

"How about wrestling alligators?"

"No . . . I always wanted to, though."

"Roller-skating down a flight of stairs?"

"No, I never thought of it."

"But you said you were *active*."

At this point, the Backson replies, thoughtfully, "I say – do you think there's something . . . *wrong* with me? Maybe I'm losing my energy."

After a while, maybe.

The Athletic sort of Backson – one of the many common varieties – is concerned with physical fitness, he says. But for some reason, he sees it as something that has to be pounded in from the outside, rather than built up from the inside. Therefore, he confuses exercise with *work*. He works when he works, works when he exercises, and, more often than not, works when he plays. Work, work, work. All work and no play makes Backson a dull boy. Kept up for long enough, it makes him dead, too.

Well – here's Rabbit. "Hello, Rabbit. What's new?"

"I just got back from Owl's," said Rabbit, slightly out of breath.

"Oh? You were certainly gone a long time."

"Yes, well . . . Owl insisted on telling me a story about his Great-Uncle Philbert."

"Oh, *that's* why."

"But anyway — Owl said that he hasn't seen the Uncarved Block, either, but that Roo is probably playing with it. So I stopped off at Kanga's house, but no one was there."

"They're out in the Forest, practicing jumps with Tigger," I said.

"Oh. Well, I'd better be going, then."

"That's all right, Rabbit, because — "

Where'd he go? That's how it is, you know — no rest for the Backson.

Let's put it this way: if you want to be healthy, relaxed, and contented, just watch what a Bisy Backson does and then do the opposite. There's one now, pacing back and forth, jingling the loose coins in his pocket, nervously glancing at his watch. He makes you feel tired just looking at him. The chronic Backson always seems to have to be *going* somewhere, at least on a superficial, physical level. He doesn't go out for a *walk*, though; he doesn't have time.

"Not conversing," said Eeyore. "Not first one and then the other. You said 'Hallo' and Flashed Past. I saw your tail in the distance as I was meditating my reply. I *had* thought of saying 'What?' – but, of course, it was then too late."

"Well, I was in a hurry."

"No Give and Take," Eeyore went on. "No Exchange of Thought: '*Hallo – What*' – I mean, it gets you nowhere, particularly if the other person's tail is only just in sight for the second half of the conversation."

The Bisy Backson is always On The Run, it seems, always:

GONE OUT

BACK SOON

BUSY

BACK SOON

or, more accurately:

BACK OUT

GONE SOON

BUSY

GONE SOON

The Bisy Backson is always going *somewhere*, somewhere he hasn't been. Anywhere but where he is.

> "That's just it," said Rabbit, "Where?"
>
> "Perhaps he's looking for something."
>
> "What?" asked Rabbit.
>
> "That's just what I was going to say," said Pooh. And then he added, "Perhaps he's looking for a – for a – "

For a Reward, perhaps. Our Bisy Backson religions, sciences, and business ethics have tried their hardest to convince us that there is a Great Reward waiting for us somewhere, and that what we have to do is spend our lives working like lunatics to catch up with it. Whether it's up in the sky, behind the next molecule, or in the executive suite, it's somehow always farther along than we are – just down the road, on the other side of the world, past the moon, beyond the stars. . . .

"Ouch!" said Pooh, landing on the floor.

"That's what happens when you go to sleep on the edge of the writing table," I said. "You fall off."

"Just as well," said Pooh.

"Why's that?" I asked.

"I was having an awful dream," he said.

"Oh?"

"Yes. I'd found a jar of honey . . .," he said, rubbing his eyes.

"What's awful about that?" I asked.

"It kept moving," said Pooh. "They're not supposed to do that. They're *supposed* to sit still."

"Yes, I know."

"But whenever I reached for it, this jar of honey would sort of go somewhere else."

"A nightmare," I said.

"Lots of people have dreams like that," I added reassuringly.

"Oh," said Pooh. "About Unreachable jars of honey?"

"About the same sort of thing," I said. "That's not unusual. The odd thing, though, is that some people *live* like that."

"Why?" asked Pooh.

"I don't know," I said. "I suppose because it gives them Something to Do."

"It doesn't sound like much fun to me," said Pooh.

No, it doesn't. A way of life that keeps saying, "Around the next corner, above the next step," works against the natural order of things and makes it so difficult to be happy and good that only a few get to where they would naturally have been in the first place – Happy and Good – and the rest give up and fall by the side of the road, cursing the world, which is not to blame but which is there to help show the way.

Those who think that the rewarding things in life are somewhere beyond the rainbow –

"Burn their toast a lot," said Pooh.

"I beg your pardon?"

"They burn their toast a lot," said Pooh.

"They – well, yes. And not only that – "

"Here comes Rabbit," said Pooh.

"Oh, there you are," said Rabbit.

"Here we are," said Pooh.

"Yes, here we are," I said.

"And there *you* are," said Pooh.

"Yes, here I am," said Rabbit impatiently. "To come to the point – Roo showed me his set of blocks. They're all carved and painted, with letters on them."

"Oh?" I said.

"Just the sort of thing you'd *expect* to see, actually," said Rabbit, stroking his whiskers thoughtfully. "So by process of elimination," he said, "that means *Eeyore* has it."

"But Rabbit," I said. "You see – "

"Yes," said Rabbit. "I see Eeyore and find out what

he knows about it – that's clearly the next step."

"There he goes," said Pooh.

Looking back a few years, we see that the first Bisy Backsons in this part of the world, the Puritans, practically worked themselves to death in the fields without getting much of anything in return for their tremendous efforts. They were actually starving until the wiser inhabitants of the land showed them a few things about working in harmony with the earth's rhythms. Now you plant; now you relax. Now you work the soil; now you leave it alone. The Puritans never really understood the second half, never really believed in it. And so, after two or three centuries of pushing, pushing, and pushing the once-fertile earth, and a few years of depleting its energy still further with synthetic stimulants, we have apples that taste like cardboard, oranges that taste like tennis balls, and pears that taste like sweetened Styrofoam, all products of soil that is not allowed to relax. We're not supposed to complain, but There It Is.

"I say, Pooh, why aren't *you* busy?" I said.

"Because it's a nice day," said Pooh.

"Yes, but – "

"Why ruin it?" he said.

"But you could be doing something Important," I said.

"I am," said Pooh.

"Oh? Doing what?"

"Listening," he said.

"Listening to what?"

"To the birds. And that squirrel over there."

"What are they saying?" I asked.

"That it's a nice day," said Pooh.

"But you know that already," I said.

"Yes, but it's always good to hear that somebody else thinks so, too," he replied.

"Well, you could be spending your time getting Educated by listening to the Radio, instead," I said.

"That thing?"

"Certainly. How else will you know what's going on in the world?" I said.

"By going outside," said Pooh.

"Er . . . well . . ." (Click.) "Now just listen to this, Pooh."

"*Thirty thousand people were killed today when five jumbo airliners collided over downtown Los Angeles . . . ,*" the Radio announced.

"What does *that* tell you about the world?" asked Pooh.

"Hmm. You're right." (Click.)

"What are the birds saying now?" I asked.

"That it's a nice day," said Pooh.

It certainly is, even if the Backsons *are* too busy to enjoy it. But to conclude our explanation of why so busy . . .

The hardheaded followers of the previously mentioned Party-Crashing Busybody religion failed to appreciate the beauty of the endless forest and clear waters that appeared before them on the fresh green continent of the New World. Instead, they saw the paradise that was there and the people who lived in harmony with it as alien and threatening, something to attack and conquer — because it all stood in the way of the Great Reward. They didn't like singing very much, either. In fact —

"What?" said Pooh. "No singing?"

"Pooh, I'm trying to finish this. That's right, though. No singing. They didn't like it."

"Well, if they didn't like singing, then what was their attitude towards Bears?"

"I don't think they liked Bears, either."

"They didn't like *Bears*?"

"No. Not very much, anyway."

"No singing, no Bears . . . Just what *did* they like?"

"I don't think they liked *anything*, Pooh."

"No wonder things are a little Confused around here," he said.

Anyway, from the Miserable Puritan came the Restless Pioneer, and from him, the Lonely Cowboy, always riding off into the sunset, looking for something just down the trail. From this rootless, dissatisfied ancestry has come the Bisy Backson, who, like his forefathers, has never really felt at home, at peace, with this Friendly Land. Rigid, combative fanatic that he is, the tightfisted Backson is just too hard on himself, too hard on others, and too hard on the world that heroically attempts to carry on in spite of what he is doing to it.

It's not surprising, therefore, that the Backson thinks of progress in terms of fighting and overcoming. One of his little idiosyncrasies, you might say. Of course, *real* progress involves growing and developing, which involves changing inside, but that's something the inflexible Backson is unwilling to do. The urge to grow and develop, present in all forms of life, becomes perverted in the Bisy Backson's mind into a constant struggle to change everything (the Bulldozer Backson) and everyone (the Bigoted Backson) else *but* himself, and interfere with things he has no business interfering with, including practically every form of life on earth. At least to a limited extent, his behavior has been held in check by wiser people around him. But, like parents of hyperactive children, the wise find that they can't be everywhere at once. Baby-sitting the Backsons wears you out.

"Here's Rabbit again," said Pooh. "And Eeyore."

"Oh – Rabbit," I said.

"*And* Eeyore," said Eeyore.

"I asked Eeyore –," said Rabbit.

"That's me," said Eeyore. "Eeyore."

"Yes, I remember," I said. "I saw you just last year, out in the Swamp somewhere."

"*Swamp?*" said Eeyore indignantly. "It's not a Swamp. It's a *Bog.*"

"Swamp, Bog. . . ."

"What's a Bog?" asked Pooh.

"If your ankles get wet, that's a Bog," said Eeyore.

"I see," said Pooh.

"Whereas," continued Eeyore, "if you sink in up to your *neck*, that's a Swamp."

"Swamp, indeed," he added bitterly. "Ha!"

"Anyway, I asked Eeyore," said Rabbit, "and he said he didn't have the slightest idea what I was talking about."

"It appears that I'm not alone in that," put in Eeyore. "You don't have the slightest idea, either. Obviously."

"Just what *is* the Uncarved Block?" asked Rabbit.

"It's me," said Pooh.

"*You?*" said Eeyore. "I came all the way over here . . ."

"From the Swamp," I added helpfully.

". . . from the *Bog*, to see *Pooh*?"

"Why not?" asked Pooh.

"Anything for Rabbit to keep busy over," said Eeyore sarcastically. "Anything at all, apparently."

Now, one thing that seems rather odd to us is that the Bisy Backson Society, which practically worships youthful energy, appearance, and attitudes, has developed no effective methods of retaining them, a lack testified to by an ever-increasing reliance on the unnatural False Front approach of cosmetics and plastic surgery. Instead, it has developed countless ways of breaking youthfulness down and destroying it. Those damaging activities that are not part of the search for the Great Reward seem to accumulate under the general heading of Saving Time.

For an example of the latter, let's take a classic monument to the Bisy Backson: the Hamburger Stand.

In China, there is the Teahouse. In France, there is the Sidewalk Café. Practically every civilized country in the world has some sort of equivalent – a place where people can go to eat, relax, and talk things

over without worrying about what time it is, and
without having to leave as soon as the food is eaten.
In China, for example, the Teahouse is a real social
institution. Throughout the day, families, neighbors,
and friends drop in for tea and light food. They stay
as long as they like. Discussions may last for hours. It
would be a bit strange to call the Teahouse the non-
exclusive neighborhood social club; such terms are
too Western. But that can roughly describe part of
the function, at least from our rather compart-
mentalized point of view. "You're important. Relax
and enjoy yourself." That's the message of the
Teahouse.

What's the message of the Hamburger Stand?
Quite obviously, it's: "You don't count; hurry up."

Not only that, but as everyone knows by now, the
horrible Hamburger Stand is an insult to the cus-
tomer's health as well. Unfortunately, this is not the
only example supported by the Saving Time mentality.
We could also list the Supermarket, the Microwave
Oven, the Nuclear Power Plant, the Poisonous
Chemicals. . . .

Practically speaking, if timesaving devices really
saved time, there would be more time available to us
now than ever before in history. But, strangely enough,
we seem to have less time than even a few years ago.
It's really great fun to go somewhere where there are

no timesaving devices because, when you do, you find that you have *lots of time*. Elsewhere, you're too busy working to pay for machines to save you time so you won't have to work so hard.

The main problem with this great obsession for Saving Time is very simple: you can't *save* time. You can only spend it. But you can spend it wisely or foolishly. The Bisy Backson has practically no time at all, because he's too busy wasting it by trying to save it. And by trying to save every bit of it, he ends up wasting the whole thing.

Henry David Thoreau put it this way, in *Walden*:

> Why should we live with such hurry and waste of life? We are determined to be starved before we are hungry. Men say that a stitch in time saves nine, and so they take a thousand stitches today to save nine tomorrow.

For colorful contrast with the youth-destroying Bisy Backson Society, let's get back to Taoism for a moment. One of the most intriguing things about Taoism is that it not only contains respect for the old and wise, but also for the figure known as the Youthful Immortal. The Taoist tradition is filled with fascinating stories (fiction) and accounts (fact, embellished or otherwise) of those who, while still young, discovered the Secrets of Life. However the discoveries were made, the result in each case was the same: a long life of youthful appearance, outlook, and energy.

For that matter, Taoist Immortals of all age levels have traditionally been known for their young attitudes, appearances, and energies. These were hardly accidental, but resulted from Taoist practices. For centuries in China, the general life expectancy was not much more than forty years, and hardworking farmers and dissipated aristocrats often died even younger than that. Yet countless Taoists lived into their eighties and nineties, and many lived considerably longer. The following is one of our favorite examples.

In 1933, newspapers around the world announced the death of a man named Li Chung Yun. As officially and irrefutably recorded by the Chinese government, and as verified by a thorough independent investigation, Li had been born in 1677. When over the age of two hundred, he had given a series of twenty-eight, three-hour-long talks on longevity at a Chinese university. Those who saw him at that time claimed that he looked like a man in his fifties, standing straight and tall, with strong teeth and a full head of hair. When he died, he was two hundred fifty-six years old.

When Li was a child, he left home to follow some wandering herbalists. In the mountains of China, he learned from them some of the secrets of the earth's medicine. In addition to using various rejuvenative herbs daily, he practiced Taoist exercises, believing that exercise which strains and tires the mind and body shortens life. His favorite way of traveling was what he called "walking lightly." Young men who went for walks with him when he was in his later years could not match his pace, which he maintained for miles. He advised those who wanted strong health to "sit like a turtle, walk like a pigeon, and sleep like a dog." When asked for his major secret, though, he would reply, "inner quiet."

Speaking of that sort of thing, let's return to *The House at Pooh Corner*. Christopher Robin has just asked Pooh a question:

> "What do you like doing best in the world, Pooh?"
>
> "Well," said Pooh, "what I like best — " and then he had to stop and think. Because although Eating Honey *was* a very good thing to do, there was a moment just before you began to eat it which was better than when you were, but he didn't know what it was called.

The honey doesn't taste so good once it is being eaten; the goal doesn't mean so much once it is reached; the reward is not so rewarding once it has been given. If we add up all the rewards in our lives, we won't have very much. But if we add up the spaces *between* the rewards, we'll come up with quite a bit. And if we add up the rewards *and* the spaces, then we'll have everything − every minute of the time that we spent. What if we could enjoy it?

The Christmas presents once opened are Not So Much Fun as they were while we were in the process of examining, lifting, shaking, thinking about, and opening them. Three hundred sixty-five days later, we try again and find that the same thing has happened. Each time the goal is reached, it becomes Not So Much Fun, and we're off to reach the next one, then the next one, then the next.

That doesn't mean that the goals we have don't count. They do, mostly because they cause us to go through the process, and it's the *process* that makes us wise, happy, or whatever. If we do things in the wrong sort of way, it makes us miserable, angry, confused, and things like that. The goal has to be right for us, and it has to be beneficial, in order to ensure a beneficial process. But aside from that, it's really the process that's important. *Enjoyment* of the process is the secret that erases the myths of the Great Reward and Saving Time. Perhaps this can help to explain the everyday significance of the word *Tao*, the Way.

What could we call that moment before we begin to eat the honey? Some would call it anticipation, but we think it's more than that. We would call it awareness. It's when we become happy and realize it, if only for an instant. By Enjoying the Process, we can stretch that awareness out so that it's no longer only a moment, but covers the whole thing. Then we can have a lot of fun. Just like Pooh.

> And then he thought that being with Christopher Robin was a very good thing to do, and having Piglet near was a very friendly thing to have; and so, when he had thought it all out, he said, "What I like best in the whole world is Me and Piglet going to see You, and You saying "What about a little something?" and Me saying, "Well, I shouldn't mind a little something, should you, Piglet," and it being a hummy sort of day outside, and birds singing."

When we take the time to enjoy our surroundings and appreciate being alive, we find that we have no time to be Bisy Backsons anymore. But that's all right, because being Bisy Backsons is a tremendous waste of time. As the poet Lu Yu wrote:

> *The clouds above us join and separate,*
> *The breeze in the courtyard leaves and returns.*
> *Life is like that, so why not relax?*
> *Who can stop us from celebrating?*

That Sort of Bear

We were discussing the "Ode to Joy," the choral finale to Beethoven's Ninth Symphony.

"It's one of my favorites," said Pooh.

"Same here," I said.

"My favorite part," said Pooh, "is where they go:

Sing Ho! for the life of a Bear!"

"But – "

"Sing Ho! for a Bear!
Sing Ho! for a Pooh!"

"But they don't – "

"Sing Ho! for the life of a Bear!"

"My favorite part," he added.

"But they don't *sing*, 'Sing Ho! for the life of a Bear!' in the 'Ode to Joy,' " I said.

"They don't?"

"No, they don't."

"Why not?"

"Well, because they hadn't *thought* of it, I guess."

"They *what?*"

"Neither Ludwig van Beethoven nor the man who wrote the words of the 'Ode to Joy' put anything in it about Bears."

"Oh. I must have been thinking of Ludwig van *Bear*thoven."

"Pooh, there *is* no Ludwig van Bearthoven. You wrote that song yourself."

"I did?"

"That's right."

"Oh, so *that's* where I heard it," he said.

But anyway, that brings us to what we're going to discuss here – enjoying life and being Special. Everyone *is* Special, you know.

> "It is hard to be brave," said Piglet, sniffing slightly, "when you're only a Very Small Animal."

Rabbit, who had begun to write very busily, looked up and said:

"It is because you are a very small animal that you will be Useful in the adventure before us."

Piglet was so excited at the idea of being Useful that he forgot to be frightened any more, and when Rabbit went on to say that Kangas were only Fierce during the winter months, being at other times of an Affectionate Disposition, he could hardly sit still, he was so eager to begin being useful at once.

"What about me?" said Pooh sadly. "I suppose *I* shan't be useful?"

"Never mind, Pooh," said Piglet comfortingly. "Another time perhaps."

"Without Pooh," said Rabbit solemnly as he sharpened his pencil, "the adventure would be impossible."

"Oh!" said Piglet, and tried not to look disappointed. But Pooh went into a corner of the room and said proudly to himself, "Impossible without Me! *That* sort of Bear."

No matter how Useful we may be, sometimes it takes us a while to recognize our own value. This can be illustrated by the Chinese story of *The Stonecutter*.

There was once a stonecutter, who was dissatisfied with himself and with his position in life.

One day, he passed a wealthy merchant's house, and through the open gateway, saw many fine possessions and important visitors. "How powerful that merchant must be!" thought the stonecutter. He became very envious, and wished that he could be like the merchant. Then he would no longer have to live the life of a mere stonecutter.

To his great surprise, he suddenly became the merchant, enjoying more luxuries and power than he had ever dreamed of, envied and detested by those less wealthy than himself. But soon a high official passed by, carried in a sedan chair, accompanied by attendants, and escorted by soldiers beating gongs. Everyone, no matter how wealthy, had to bow low before the procession. "How powerful that official is!" he thought. "I wish that *I* could be a high official!"

Then he became the high official, carried everywhere in his embroidered sedan chair, feared and hated by the people all around, who had to bow down before him as he passed. It was a hot summer day, and the official felt very uncomfortable in the sticky sedan chair. He looked up at the sun. It shone proudly in the sky, unaffected by his presence. "How powerful the sun is!" he thought. "I wish that *I* could be the sun!"

Then he became the sun, shining fiercely down

on everyone, scorching the fields, cursed by the farmers and laborers. But a huge black cloud moved between him and the earth, so that his light could no longer shine on everything below. "How powerful that storm cloud is!" he thought. "I wish that *I* could be a cloud!"

Then he became the cloud, flooding the fields and villages, shouted at by everyone. But soon he found that he was being pushed away by some great force, and realized that it was the wind. "How powerful it is!" he thought. "I wish that *I* could be the wind!"

Then he became the wind, blowing tiles off the roofs of houses, uprooting trees, hated and feared by all below him. But after a while, he ran up against something that would not move, no matter how forcefully he blew against it – a huge, towering stone. "How powerful that stone is!" he thought. I wish that *I* could be a stone!"

Then he became the stone, more powerful than anything else on earth. But as he stood there, he heard the sound of a hammer pounding a chisel into the solid rock, and felt himself being changed. "What could be more powerful than I, the stone?" he thought. He looked down and saw far below him the figure of a stonecutter.

Ah, here's the mail. "Oh, look – something for you, Pooh."

"For *me*?" said Pooh.

"For Mister Pooh Bear."

"*Mister* Pooh Bear?"

"That's what it says."

"Mister . . . Pooh . . . Bear," said Pooh in an awed sort of voice. "What's it say?" he asked, climbing onto the writing table and looking over my shoulder.

"It's from Finchley's. '*Announcing our third annual shoe sale. All styles, all sizes.*' Pooh, you don't need this."

"What's that say at the bottom?" asked Pooh.

" 'Free Coffee.' One more reason to stay away."

"Let me examine this more carefully," said Pooh, taking it over by the window.

In order to take control of our lives and accomplish something of lasting value, sooner or later we need to learn to Believe. We don't need to shift our responsibilities onto the shoulders of some deified Spiritual Superman, or sit around and wait for Fate to come knocking at the door. We simply need to believe in the power that's within us, and use it. When we do that, and stop imitating others and competing against them, things begin to work for us.

Let's take a couple of examples:

In 1927, a thirty-two-year-old man stood on the edge of the lake in Chicago's Lincoln Park, planning to drop beneath the dark waters and drown. His daughter had died, his company had gone bankrupt, his reputation had been ruined, and he was becoming an alcoholic. Looking into the lake, he asked himself what one small man in his position could possibly do. Then an answer came to him: he was now free to take risks, to initiate action on his own, and, by doing so, to help other people. He returned home and committed himself to the work that he believed the universe wanted him to do, instead of what he had been *taught* to do. He watched the laws of the natural world and altered his own living patterns accordingly, eventually changing his life completely. Those laws were to inspire and support him in his greatest achievements. But without his believing and taking a chance, his contributions to humanity would never have been made, and no one would have come to respect the name of Buckminster Fuller.

In 1854, a boy was withdrawn from school in Port Huron, Michigan, for "causing trouble." He had been there for three months. That was to be the only formal education of his life. He later worked as a laboratory assistant. The job ended when he blew up the laboratory. His employer picked him up and threw him out into the dust, saying that he would never amount to anything. But he had a plan, and he wasn't going to let a little problem or two stop him. He wanted to learn the mechanical applications of natural laws. He eventually became the foremost inventor in American history, with over thirteen hundred domestic and foreign patents registered in his name, a name synonymous with problem-solving genius, the name of Thomas Edison.

The play-it-safe pessimists of the world never accomplish much of anything, because they don't look clearly and objectively at situations, they don't recognize or believe in their own abilities, and they won't stretch those abilities to overcome even the smallest amount of risk. For example, when Roo fell into the stream during the famous Expedition to find the North Pole, what did Dismal Eeyore do about it? Long after Roo had been carried away by the current, Eeyore halfheartedly hung his tail over the water so that Roo could grab hold of it and pull himself out — or, more accurately, so that Eeyore would get credit for having tried something. Of course, he didn't really expect it to do any good, and of course it didn't.

Who was going to rescue Roo? Panicky Piglet was jumping up and down and making noises. Ineffective Owl was instructing Roo to keep his head above water. Concerned Kanga was asking if he was all right. Captain Rabbit was calling out commands. . . . But Positive Pooh was looking at the situation, seeing what he could do about it, and trying something:

Two pools below Roo he was standing with a long pole in his paws, and Kanga came up and took one end of it, and between them they held it across the lower part of the pool; and Roo, still bubbling proudly, "Look at me swimming," drifted up against it, and climbed out.

"Did you see me swimming?" squeaked Roo excitedly, while Kanga scolded him and rubbed him down. "Pooh, did you see me swimming? That's called swimming, what I was doing. Rabbit, did you see what I was doing? Swimming. Hallo, Piglet! I say, Piglet! What do you think I was doing! Swimming! Christopher Robin, did you see me — "

But Christopher Robin wasn't listening. He was looking at Pooh.

"Pooh," he said, "where did you find that pole?"

Pooh looked at the pole in his hands.

"I just found it," he said. "I thought it ought to be useful. I just picked it up."

"Pooh," said Christopher Robin solemnly, "the Expedition is over. You have found the North Pole!"

As Pooh found out with the North Pole, once we see what the situation is and what we can do about it, we need to utilize everything we find along the way in order to accomplish whatever is required. More often than not, the things we need are there already; all we have to do is make use of them.

For example, when Piglet was Trapped by the Flood . . .

"It's a little Anxious," he said to himself, "to be a Very Small Animal Entirely Surrounded by Water. Christopher Robin and Pooh could escape by Climbing Trees, and Kanga could escape by Jumping, and Rabbit could escape by Burrowing, and Owl could escape by Flying, and Eeyore could escape by – by Making a Loud Noise Until Rescued, and here am I, surrounded by water and I can't do *anything*. . . ."

Then suddenly he remembered a story which Christopher Robin had told him about a man on a desert island who had written something in a bottle and thrown it in the sea; and Piglet

thought that if he wrote something in a bottle
and threw it in the water, perhaps somebody
would come and rescue *him*!

So he did.

And when Piglet's bottle came floating past him,
Pooh got the message. But then he had to go see
Christopher Robin in order to find out what it *said*.

So he corked up his biggest honey-jar, dropped it
into the water, and jumped in after it. And after a
little experimenting with his boat,

he floated off to Christopher Robin's house, where
the message was read and a Rescue planned. Then
the two of them realized that they needed a larger
boat. So Pooh got an idea:

And in an exciting Rescue, Piglet was saved by none
other than the famous Pooh Bear, Discoverer of the
North Pole.

"Say, Owl. Have you seen Pooh lately?"

"I rather thought I saw him putting something into the closet a little while ago," Owl replied. "I wasn't paying much attention to the matter, though."

"The closet? Well, I'll just take a look and – "

"What is it?" said Owl.

"Owl, *what* are all these boxes doing in here?"

"Boxes?" said Owl.

"And they're all full of . . . *shoes*."

"Shoes?" said Owl.

"Look at this. Loafers, 8½ A. Sandals, 10 B. Oxfords, 12½ E . . ."

"All styles, all sizes," said Owl.

"Owl, I'm not quite sure, but I believe I Suspect something."

"It would appear that *Pooh* is the culprit," said Owl wisely.

"When you see him, tell him I want to talk with him, will you, Owl?"

"Absolutely."

The two Fearless Rescues just mentioned bring us to one of the most important terms of Taoism: *Tz'u*, which can be translated as "caring" or "compassion" and which is based upon the character for *heart*. In the sixty-seventh chapter of the *Tao Te Ching*, Lao-tse named it as his "first treasure," and then wrote,

"From caring comes courage." We might add that from it also comes wisdom. It's rather significant, we think, that those who have no compassion have no wisdom. Knowledge, yes; cleverness, maybe; wisdom, no. A clever mind is not a heart. Knowledge doesn't really care. Wisdom does. We also consider it significant that *cor*, the Latin word for "heart," is the basis for the word *courage*. Piglet put it this way: "She isn't Clever, Kanga isn't, but she would be so anxious about Roo that she would do a Good Thing to Do without thinking about it." *Tz'u* not only saved Roo, discovered the North Pole, and rescued Piglet; it also gave Piglet the courage to go get help for Pooh and Owl when Owl's house blew over.

Now Piglet, as we know, is a Very Small Animal, and not exactly the *Bravest* one at that, but when Owl's house fell down, Piglet discovered that he had more courage than he had *thought* he had.

> "Hallo, Owl," said Pooh. "I hope we're not too late for – I mean, how are you, Owl? Piglet and I just came to see how you were, because it's Thursday."
>
> "Sit down, Pooh, sit down, Piglet," said Owl kindly. "Make yourselves comfortable."
>
> They thanked him, and made themselves as comfortable as they could.

"Because, you see, Owl," said Pooh, "we've been hurrying, so as to be in time for — so as to see you before we went away again."

Owl nodded solemnly.

"Correct me if I am wrong," he said, "but am I right in supposing that it is a very Blusterous day outside?"

"Very," said Piglet, who was quietly thawing his ears, and wishing that he was safely back in his own house.

"I thought so," said Owl. "It was on just such a blusterous day as this that my Uncle Robert, a portrait of whom you see upon the wall on your right, Piglet, while returning in the late forenoon from a — What's that?"

There was a loud cracking noise.

"Look out!" cried Pooh. "Mind the clock! Out of the way, Piglet! Piglet, I'm falling on you!"

"Help!" cried Piglet. . . .

"Pooh," said Piglet nervously.

"Yes?" said one of the chairs.

"Where are we?"

"I'm not quite sure," said the chair.

"Are we — are we in Owl's House?"

"I think so, because we were just going to have tea, and we hadn't had it."

"Oh!" said Piglet. "Well, did Owl *always* have a letter-box in his ceiling?"

But after the chair was pulled off of Pooh and he had taken a look around, he came up with a Plan. Owl would fly up to the letter-box with a piece of string, push the string through the wire in the basket, and fly down again. Then Piglet would hold onto one end of the string while Pooh and Owl pulled on the other end . . .

"And there Piglet is," said Owl. "If the string doesn't break."

"Supposing it does?" asked Piglet, wanting to know.

"Then we try another piece of string."

This was not very comforting to Piglet, because however many pieces of string they tried pulling him up with, it would always be the same him coming down; but still, it did seem the only thing to do. So with one last look back in his mind at all the happy hours he had spent in the Forest *not* being pulled up to the ceiling by a piece of string, Piglet nodded bravely at Pooh and said that it was a Very Clever pup-pup-pup Clever pup-pup Plan.

And at last . . .

He squeezed and he squoze, and then with one last sqooze he was out. Happy and excited he turned round to squeak a last message to the prisoners.

"It's all right," he called through the letter-box. "Your tree is blown right over, Owl, and there's a branch across the door, but Christopher Robin and I can move it, and we'll bring a rope for Pooh, and I'll go and tell him now, and I can climb down quite easily, I mean it's dangerous but I can do it all right, and Christopher Robin and I will be back in about half-an-hour. Good-bye, Pooh!" And without waiting to hear Pooh's answering "Good-bye, and thank you, Piglet," he was off.

"Half-an-hour," said Owl, settling himself comfortably. "That will just give me time to finish that story I was telling you about my Uncle Robert – a portrait of whom you see underneath you. Now let me see, where was I? Oh, yes. It was on just such a blusterous day as this that my Uncle Robert – "

"Owl said you wanted to see me," said Pooh.

"All right, Pooh. Why the boxes of shoes in the closet?"

"I couldn't help myself," said Pooh.

"How's that?"

"Well, first there was the card for *Mister* Pooh Bear. Then when I got to the store, just for a look . . ."

"Yes?"

"The salesman was so *nice* to me. 'May I help you, Sir?' he said. He made me feel Important."

"Pooh, you didn't *need* those shoes," I said.

"I'll take them back," said Pooh.

"That's better."

"Lots of other people will be taking things back, too, I suppose."

"What?"

"I saw lots of people there buying things they

didn't really need. All over the store."

"Quite likely," I said.

"I wasn't the only one," he said.

"Of course not, Pooh. A lot of people try to buy Happiness and Importance in the same sort of way. But *you* can be happy and important without doing that, you know."

"So can they," said Pooh.

Well, yes, that's true. So can anyone. Despite what Eeyore once said, when it comes to enjoying life and making use of who we are, all of us *can*; it's just that some *don't*.

Sitting contented by Walden Pond a few years ago, a Wise Observer wrote, "The mass of men lead lives of quiet desperation." The desperation may have been quiet *then*, we suppose. *Now*, it's deafening. But we don't have to be a part of it. We can stop our desperate clinging to hollow life-substitutes, and set ourselves free. When we make the first move, the process will begin.

And that brings us to the Tiddely-Pom Principle, which comes from a song by Pooh:

> *The more it snows*
>   *(Tiddely pom),*
> *The more it goes*
>   *(Tiddely pom),*

The more it goes
          (Tiddely pom)
On snowing.

It's sometimes referred to as the Snowball Effect, which can remind you of the time you pushed that little ball of snow along, and it got bigger and bigger until it got so big you couldn't stop it, and it rolled all the way down the hill and flattened the neighbor's car, and soon everyone was talking about the Huge Snowball that *you* let get completely out of control . . . and that may be why we prefer to think of it as the Tiddely-Pom Principle, instead.

Now the principle can work negatively or positively. It can promote cynicism as easily as it can encourage hope. It can build hardened criminals or courageous heroes, stupid vandals or brilliant creators. The important thing is to make it work for yourself and for the benefit of others, or face the Ugly Consequences.

Working with the Tiddely-Pom Principle, you use respect to build Respect. The more it snows, the more it goes:

So Pooh hummed it to him, all the seven verses and Piglet said nothing, but just stood and glowed. Never before had anyone sung ho for

Piglet (PIGLET) ho all by himself. When it was
over, he wanted to ask for one of the verses
over again, but didn't quite like to. It was the
verse beginning "O gallant Piglet," and it
seemed to him a very thoughtful way of beginning a piece of poetry.

"Did I really do all that?" he said at last.

"Well," said Pooh, "in poetry — in a piece of
poetry — well, you *did* it, Piglet, because the
poetry says you did. And that's how people know."

"Oh!" said Piglet. "Because I — I thought I did
blinch a little. Just at first. And it says, 'Did he
blinch no no.' That's why."

"You only blinched inside," said Pooh, "and that's
the bravest way for a Very Small Animal not to
blinch that there is." Piglet sighed with happiness,
and began to think about himself. He was
BRAVE. . . .

So that later, when Uninformed Eeyore discovered
a new house for Owl to move into, and it turned out
to be *Piglet's* . . .

"Just the house for Owl. Don't you think so, little
Piglet?"

And then Piglet did a Noble Thing, and he did
it in a sort of dream, while he was thinking of all

the wonderful words Pooh had hummed about him.

"Yes, it's just the house for Owl," he said grandly. "And I hope he'll be very happy in it." And then he gulped twice, because he had been very happy in it himself.

"What do *you* think, Christopher Robin?" asked Eeyore a little anxiously, feeling that something wasn't quite right.

Christopher Robin had a question to ask first, and he was wondering how to ask it.

"Well," he said at last, "it's a very nice house, and if your own house is blown down, you *must* go somewhere else, mustn't you, Piglet? What would *you* do, if *your* house was blown down?"

Before Piglet could think, Pooh answered for him.

"He'd come and live with me," said Pooh, "wouldn't you, Piglet?"

Piglet squeezed his paw.

"Thank you, Pooh," he said, "I should love to."

Do you want to be really happy? You can begin by being appreciative of who you are and what you've got. Do you want to be really miserable? You can begin by being discontented. As Lao-tse wrote, "A tree as big around as you can reach starts with a small

seed; a thousand-mile journey starts with one step."
Wisdom, Happiness, and Courage are not waiting
somewhere out beyond sight at the end of a straight
line; they're part of a continuous cycle that begins
right here. They're not only the ending, but the
beginning as well. The more it snows, the more it
goes, the more it goes on snowing.

Chuang-tse described it this way:

> It is widely recognized that the courageous spirit
> of a single man can inspire to victory an army of
> thousands. If one concerned with ordinary gain
> can create such an effect, how much more will
> be produced by one who cares for greater things!

(Applause.) A Toast! To Gallant Piglet and Fearless
Pooh —

> *Sing ho! for Piglet (PIGLET) ho!*
> *Sing ho! for Piglet, ho!*

> *and*

> *Sing Ho! for a Bear!*
> *Sing Ho! for a Pooh!*
> *Sing Ho! for the life of a Bear!*

When they had all nearly eaten enough,
Christopher Robin banged on the table with

his spoon, and everybody stopped talking and was very silent, except Roo who was just finishing a loud attack of hiccups and trying to look as if it were one of Rabbit's relations.

"This party," said Christopher Robin, "is a party because of what someone did, and we all know who it was, and it's his party, because of what he did, and I've got a present for him and here it is." Then he felt about a little and whispered, "Where is it?"

While he was looking, Eeyore coughed in an impressive way and began to speak.

"Friends," he said, "including oddments, it is a great pleasure, or perhaps I had better say it has been a pleasure so far, to see you at my party. What I did was nothing. Any of you — except Rabbit and Owl and Kanga — would have done the same. Oh, and Pooh. My remarks do not, of course, apply to Piglet and Roo, because they are too small. Any of you would have done the same. But it just happened to be Me. It was not, I need hardly say, with an idea of getting what Christopher Robin is looking for now" — and he put his front leg to his mouth and said in a loud whisper, "Try under the table" — "that I did what I did — but because I feel that we should all do what we can to help. I feel that we should all — "

Yes, yes, yes. Well, anyway...

"Here it is!" cried Christopher Robin excitedly.
"Pass it down to silly old Pooh. It's for Pooh."

"For Pooh?" said Eeyore.

Of course it's for Pooh. Because he's *that* sort of
Bear.

"Just what makes *Pooh* so special, anyway?" said
Eeyore indignantly.
"Well, Eeyore, if you read the next chapter, you
may find out," I said.
"If we *must*," said Eeyore.

Nowhere and Nothing

"Where are we going?" said Pooh, hurrying after him, and wondering whether it was to be an Explore or a What-shall-I-do-about-you-know-what.

"Nowhere," said Christopher Robin.

So they began going there, and after they had walked a little way Christopher Robin said:

"What do you like doing best in the world, Pooh?"

(And of course, what Pooh liked doing best was going to Christopher Robin's house and eating, but since we've already quoted that, we don't think we need to quote it again.)

"I like that too," said Christopher Robin, "but what I like *doing* best is Nothing."

"How do you do Nothing?" asked Pooh, after he had wondered for a long time.

"Well, it's when people call out at you just as you're going off to do it, What are you going to do, Christopher Robin, and you say, Oh, nothing, and then you go and do it."

"Oh, I see," said Pooh.

"This is a nothing sort of thing that we're doing now."

"Oh, I see," said Pooh again.

"It means just going along, listening to all the things you can't hear, and not bothering."

Chuang-tse described it this way:

Consciousness wandered North to the land of the Dark Waters and climbed the Unnoticeable Slope, where he met Speechless Non-Doer. "I have three questions for you," Consciousness said. "First, what thoughts and efforts will lead us to understanding the Tao? Second, where must we go and what must we do to find peace in the Tao? Third, from what point must we start and which road must we follow in order to reach the Tao?" Speechless Non-Doer gave him no answer.

Consciousness traveled South to the land of the Bright Ocean and climbed the Mountain of Certainty, where he saw Impulsive Speech-Maker. He asked him the same questions. "Here are the answers," Impulsive Speech-Maker replied. But as soon as he started to speak, he became confused and forgot what he was talking about.

Consciousness returned to the palace and asked the Yellow Emperor, who told him, "To have no thought and put forth no effort is the first step towards understanding the Tao. To go nowhere and do nothing is the first step towards finding peace in the Tao. To start from no point and follow no road is the first step towards reaching the Tao."

What Chuang-tse, Christopher Robin, and Pooh are describing is the Great Secret, the key that unlocks the doors of wisdom, happiness, and truth. What is that magic, mysterious something? Nothing. To the Taoist, Nothing is *something*, and Something – at least the sort of thing that many consider to be important – is really nothing at all. Our explanation of this will attempt to give some sort of indication of what the Taoists call *T'ai Hsü*, the "Great Nothing."

We will begin with an illustration from the writings of Chuang-tse:

On his way back from the K'un-lun Mountains, the Yellow Emperor lost the dark pearl of Tao. He sent Knowledge to find it, but Knowledge was unable able to understand it. He sent Distant Vision, but Distant Vision was unable to see it. He sent Eloquence, but Eloquence was unable to describe it.

Finally, he sent Empty Mind, and Empty Mind came back with the pearl.

When Eeyore lost his tail, who found it for him? Clever Rabbit? No. He was busy doing Clever Things. Scholarly Owl? No. He didn't recognize it when he saw it. Know-It-All Eeyore? No. He didn't even realize that it was missing until Pooh told him. And even then, it took a while to convince him that the tail was definitely Not There.

Then Pooh went off to find it. First, he stopped at Owl's house, and Owl told him in twenty-five

thousand monotonous words or more that the Thing
To Do would be to Issue a Reward, which would
involve writing out a . . . (yawn) . . . notice, and putting
it . . . (YAWN) . . . all over the . . . (umm). Oh, yes –
where were we? All over the Forest. And then they
went outside . . .

> And Pooh looked at the knocker and the notice
> below it, and he looked at the bell-rope and the
> notice below it, and the more he looked at the
> bellrope, the more he felt that he had seen
> something like it, somewhere else, sometime
> before.
>
> "Handsome bell-rope, isn't it?" said Owl.
>
> Pooh nodded.
>
> "It reminds me of something," he said, "but I
> can't think what. Where did you get it?"
>
> "I just came across it in the Forest. It was hanging
> over a bush, and I thought at first somebody lived
> there, so I rang it, and nothing happened, and
> then I rang it again very loudly, and it came off
> in my hand, and as nobody seemed to want it, I
> took it home, and – "

Aha. So Pooh returned the tail to Eeyore, and after
it had been put back in place, Eeyore felt much better.

For a while, anyway.

An Empty sort of mind is valuable for finding pearls and tails and things because it can see what's in front of it. An Overstuffed mind is unable to. While the Clear mind listens to a bird singing, the Stuffed-Full-of-Knowledge-and-Cleverness mind wonders what *kind* of bird is singing. The more Stuffed Up it is, the less it can hear through its own ears and see through its own eyes. Knowledge and Cleverness tend to concern themselves with the wrong sorts of things, and a mind confused by Knowledge, Cleverness, and Abstract Ideas tends to go chasing off after things that don't matter, or that don't even exist, instead of seeing, appreciating, and making use of what is right in front of it.

Let's consider Emptiness in general for a moment. What is it about a Taoist landscape painting that seems so refreshing to so many different kinds of people?

The Emptiness, the space that's not filled in. What is it about fresh snow, clean air, pure water? Or good music? As Claude Debussy expressed it, "Music is the space between the notes."

"Wooh *Baby*! Oooaowee *BABY*! (Wanga wanga wanga.) Baby, don't *leave* me! (Wanga wanga crash bang!) Baby, don't *LEAVE* me!" (Click.) Like silence after noise, or cool, clear water on a hot, stuffy day, Emptiness cleans out the messy mind and charges up the batteries of spiritual energy.

Many people are afraid of Emptiness, however, because it reminds them of Loneliness. Everything has to be filled in, it seems – appointment books, hillsides, vacant lots – but when all the spaces are filled, the Loneliness *really* begins. Then the Groups are joined, the Classes are signed up for, and the Gift-to-Yourself items are bought. When the Loneliness starts creeping in the door, the Television Set is turned on to make it go away. But it doesn't go away. So some of *us* do instead, and after discarding the emptiness of the Big Congested Mess, we discover the fullness of Nothing.

One of our favorite examples of the value of Nothing is an incident in the life of the Japanese emperor Hirohito. Now, being emperor in one of the most frantically Confucianist countries in the world is not necessarily all that *relaxing*. From early morning until late at night, practically every minute of the emperor's time is filled in with meetings, audiences, tours, inspections, and who-knows-what. And through a day so tightly scheduled that it would make a stone wall seem open by comparison, the emperor must glide, like a great ship sailing in a steady breeze.

In the middle of a particularly busy day, the emperor was driven to a meeting hall for an appointment of some kind. But when he arrived, there was no one there. The emperor walked into the middle of the great hall, stood silently for a moment, then bowed to the empty space. He turned to his assistants, a large smile on his face. "We must schedule more appointments like this," he told them. "I haven't enjoyed myself so much in a long time."

In the forty-eighth chapter of the *Tao Te Ching*, Lao-tse wrote, "To attain knowledge, add things every day. To attain wisdom, remove things every day." Chuang-tse described the principle in his own humorous way:

"I am learning," Yen Hui said.

"How?" the Master asked.

"I forgot the rules of Righteousness and the levels of Benevolence," he replied.

"Good, but could be better," the Master said.

A few days later, Yen Hui remarked, "I am making progress."

"How?" the Master asked.

"I forgot the Rituals and the Music," he answered.

"Better, but not perfect," the Master said.

Some time later, Yen Hui told the Master, "Now I sit down and forget everything."

The Master looked up, startled. "What do you mean, you forget everything?" he quickly asked.

"I forget my body and senses, and leave all appearance and information behind," answered Yen Hui. "In the middle of Nothing, I join the Source of All Things."

The Master bowed. "You have transcended the limitations of time and knowledge. I am far behind you. You have found the Way!"

Gathering, analyzing, sorting, and storing information – these functions and more the mind can perform so automatically, skillfully, and effortlessly that it makes the most sophisticated computer look like a plastic toy by comparison. But it can do infinitely more. To use the mind as it's all too commonly used, on the kinds of things that it's usually used on, is about

as inefficient and inappropriate as using a magic sword
to open up a can of beans. The power of a clear mind
is beyond description. But it can be attained by anyone who can appreciate and utilize the value of
Nothing.

Let's say you get an idea – or, as Pooh would more
accurately say, it gets you. Where did it come from?
From this something, which came from *that* something? If you are able to trace it all the way back to its
source, you will discover that it came from Nothing.
And chances are, the greater the idea, the more directly
it came from there. "A stroke of genius! Completely
unheard of! A revolutionary new approach!" Practically everyone has had some sort of an idea like that
sometime, most likely after a sound sleep when
everything was so clear and filled with Nothing that
an Idea suddenly appeared in it. But we don't have to
fall asleep for a few hours for that to happen. We can
be awake, instead – *completely* awake. The process is
very natural.

It starts when we are children, helpless but aware
of things, enjoying what is around us. Then we reach
adolescence, still helpless but trying to at least *appear*
independent. When we outgrow that stage, we
become adults – self-sufficient individuals able and
mature enough to help others as we have learned to
help ourselves.

But the adult is not the highest stage of development. The end of the cycle is that of the independent, clear-minded, all-seeing Child. That is the level known as wisdom. When the *Tao Te Ching* and other wise books say things like, "Return to the beginning; become a child again," that's what they're referring to. Why do the en*light*ened seem filled with light and happiness, like children? Why do they sometimes even look and talk like children? Because they are. The wise are Children Who Know. Their minds have been emptied of the countless minute somethings of small learning, and filled with the wisdom of the Great Nothing, the Way of the Universe.

> They walked on, thinking of This and That, and by-and-by they came to an enchanted place on the very top of the Forest called Galleons Lap, which is sixty-something trees in a circle; and Christopher Robin knew that it was enchanted because nobody had ever been able to count whether it was sixty-three or sixty-four, not even when he tied a piece of string round each tree after he had counted it. Being enchanted, its floor was not like the floor of the Forest, gorse and bracken and heather, but close-set grass, quiet and smooth and green. . . . Sitting there they could see the whole world spread out until it reached the sky, and whatever there was all the world over was with them in Galleons Lap.

There the Pooh books come to an end, in the Enchanted Place at the top of the Forest. We can go there at any time. It's not far away; it's not hard to find. Just take the path to Nothing, and go Nowhere until you reach it. Because the Enchanted Place is right where you are, and if you're Friendly With Bears, you can find it.

The Now of Pooh

In the morning sunshine, in the evening twilight, a small Bear travels through a Forest. Why did we follow him when we were so much younger? He is, after all, only a Bear of Little Brain. But is Brain all that important? Is it really Brain that takes us where we need to go? Or is it all too often Brain that sends us off in the wrong direction, following the echo of the wind in the treetops, which we *think* is real, rather than listening to the voice within us that tells us which way to turn?

A Brain can do all kinds of things, but the things that it can do are not the most important things. Abstract cleverness of mind only separates the thinker from the world of reality, and that world, the Forest of Real Life, is in a desperate condition now because of too many who think too much and care too little. In spite of what many minds have thought themselves into believing, that mistake cannot continue for much longer if everything is going to survive. The one chance we have to avoid certain disaster is to change our approach, and to learn to value wisdom and contentment. These are the things that are being searched for anyway, through Knowledge and Cleverness, but they do not come from Knowledge and Cleverness. They never have, and they never will. We can no longer afford to look so desperately hard for something in the wrong way and in the wrong place. If Knowledge and Cleverness are allowed to go on wrecking things, they will before much longer destroy all life on earth as we know it, and what little may temporarily survive will not be worth looking at, even if it would somehow be possible for us to do so.

The masters of life know the Way, for they listen to the voice within them, the voice of wisdom and simplicity, the voice that reasons beyond Cleverness and knows beyond Knowledge. That voice is not just the power and property of a few, but has been given to everyone. Those who pay attention to it are too often treated as exceptions to a rule, rather than as examples of the rule in operation, a rule that can apply to anyone who makes use of it.

Within each of us there is an Owl, a Rabbit, an

Eeyore, and a Pooh. For too long, we have chosen the way of Owl and Rabbit. Now, like Eeyore, we complain about the results. But that accomplishes nothing. If we are smart, we will choose the way of Pooh. As if from far away, it calls to us with the voice of a child's mind. It may be hard to hear at times, but it is important just the same, because without it, we will never find our way through the Forest.

Backword

"Well, what do you think, Pooh?" I said.

"Think about what?" asked Pooh.

"The Tao of Pooh, of course."

"The *how* of Pooh?" asked Pooh.

"Do we have to go through *that* again?" I said.

"Go through *what* again?" asked Pooh.

"The Tao of Pooh," I said.

"What's the Tao of Pooh?"

"You know – the Uncarved Block, the Cottleston Pie Principle, the Pooh Way, *That* Sort of Bear, and all that."

"Oh," said Pooh.

"That's the Tao of Pooh," I said.

"Oh," said Pooh.

"How would *you* describe it?" I asked.

"Well . . . this just came to me," he said. "I'll sing it to you."

"All right."

"Now, then . . . (er*hum*),"

To know the Way,
We go the Way;
We do the Way
The way we do
The things we do.
It's all there in front of you,
But if you try too hard to see it,
You'll only become Confused.

I am me,
And you are you,
As you can see;
But when you do
The things that you can do,
You will find the Way,
And the Way will follow you.

"That's what *I* think it is," he said.

"*Perfect*," I said. "But you know, don't you . . ."

"Know what?" said Pooh.

"It's the same thing."

"Oh," said Pooh. "So it is."

The
Te of Piglet

For Lan Ts'ai-ho

. "It is hard to be brave," said Piglet, sniffing slightly, "when you're only a Very Small Animal."

Rabbit, who had begun to write very busily, looked up and said:

"It is because you are a very small animal that you will be Useful in the adventure before us."

Contents

What? *Another* One?

One day not long ago, I found Piglet sitting by himself
on the writing table, gazing wistfully out the window.
I asked what he was doing . . .

"Oh, just wishing," he replied.
"Wishing what?" I asked.
"Nothing, really," he said, turning pinker than
usual around the ears.
"You know I won't make fun of you if you tell
me."
"Well . . . I was only wishing – "
"Yes?"
"Only wishing . . . That someday someone would
notice me."
"*I* notice you."

"I only meant – that is, most everyone notices Pooh . . ."

"Yes, most everyone does. Ever since the Pooh books came out, years ago."

"And now, especially," said Piglet. "Because of you-know-what."

"Ah, yes," I said. "Just for a moment, I'd forgotten."

And then it was my turn to gaze wistfully out the window, remembering the spring of 1982. For it was then that Dutton released a book of mine called *The Tao of Pooh*. It seemed so long ago, somehow . . .

The Tao of Pooh began as a reaction to what I considered an unfortunate situation. English-language writings on the Chinese philosophy of Taoism – which, I had come to realize, was far more than "Chinese," and far more than "philosophy" – had for many years been dominated by scholarly sorts who seemed more interested in cataloguing and bickering over Minute Particulars than in communicating the practical wisdom of Taoist principles.

For most of my life I had been learning those principles from various Taoist teachers – some official and some not, some Chinese and some not, some in human form and (the best instructors of them all) some not. I saw them being muddled and mutilated in the "Taoist" writings of scholars who were not

Taoists, who had not been taught by Taoists, and who did not practice Taoist skills and exercises – yet who monopolized the subject of Taoism and sneered at anyone who suggested that there was more to it than what they told.

I would come across such things as a description by the Taoist writer Chuang-tse of some tactics of swordsmanship, translated into nonsense by an Authority apparently ignorant of even the basic precepts of Taoist martial arts . . . And I would ask myself if there weren't something that could be done about that sort of thing.

Then one day, while quoting to someone from A. A. Milne's *Winnie-the-Pooh*, I got an Idea. I could write a book explaining Taoism through the characters in *Winnie-the-Pooh* and *The House at Pooh Corner*. That would, it seemed to me, release Taoist wisdom from the grip of the Overacademics and restore to it the childlike awareness and sense of humor that they had taken away.

On being told of the Idea, certain Eeyores advised me against attempting anything of the sort. But following the advice of Eeyores has rarely seemed A Particularly Good Thing for Me to Do. Quite the contrary: If the Eeyores are against something, I tend to think there might be something to it.

And so I wrote the manuscript, it was published,

and that (I thought) was the end of the matter. But it wasn't. It was more or less the beginning.

Before *The Tao of Pooh*, one would not have heard many nonscholarly or nonmystical Westerners discussing Taoism. But today Taoist principles are described in publications on business, science, psychology, health, sports, music, art, writing, computer programming, and other subjects. They are discussed in corporate-strategy sessions, high school and college classes, and other gatherings of various kinds. And (according to what I've read and heard) the book most often recommended to explain Taoist principles is *The Tao of Pooh*. Colleges use the book as a text on Taoism, psychiatrists give copies to their patients, ministers quote from it in their sermons, Chinese martial arts instructors read it to their students, and so on. I have even been told that some motel owners put it in their rental units. It would seem that *The Tao of Pooh* (also known as *Le Tao de Pooh, Tao enligt Puh, Nalle Puh ja Tao*, and such) is known and liked around the world. And that, I must say, has pleased Pooh enormously.

"Oh, Pooh!" said everybody else except Eeyore.

"Thank-you," growled Pooh.

But Eeyore was saying to himself, "This writing

business. Pencils and what-not. Over-rated, if you
ask me. Silly stuff. Nothing in it."

And so *The Tao of Pooh* has become known as a
Remarkable Success. And until fairly recently, I'd
considered that The End. I'd explained Taoist principles. I'd entertained with Pooh and friends. There
were other things I wanted to do, other things I
wanted to be associated with. "Stop this Remarkable
Success, please," I asked. "I'd like to get off." But no
one wanted to let me off. "No, I don't intend a *Tao of
Pooh* sequel. I don't like sequels. Thank you very much.
Good-bye."
But slowly and softly — so softly that for a long
time I was unaware of it — something began to steal
into my consciousness. A small voice was trying to
catch my attention. After a while, I realized that it
was Piglet's. Finally I sat down and listened. And after
listening for a while, I began to take notes . . . There
was more to be said, Piglet pointed out — but no one
was saying it, and it was needed today. It would be
needed even more, he said, in the years to come.
Another book needn't be a "sequel"; it could be a
companion book, as *The House at Pooh Corner* is to
Winnie-the-Pooh. Why did I listen to Piglet? The
answer lies in the past.
In my childhood, when the *Pooh* stories were first

read to me, I immediately developed a fondness for Piglet — from the beginning, he was my favorite of the *Pooh* characters. That I knew, but I didn't know why. By now I know why. And I hope that before you have finished reading this book, you will know why, too.

Interjection

We had wanted to make this the Introduction, but something else managed to put itself ahead of it. So we decided that we couldn't call this an Introduction, after all.

We asked Owl, who's the one to consult in matters of this sort, what one calls an Introduction that comes after something else. "An Interjection," he knowingly replied. And since Owl says that this is an Interjection, that is what it is.

Now, the first thing –

"Am *I* in it?" asked Pooh.

"Oh – Pooh. I didn't know you were here."

"Hardly anyone ever seems to notice," said Pooh sadly.

"Of course you're in it, Pooh. Now."

"That's good," he said, cheering up considerably.

What we want to explain in this Interjection —

"This *what?*" asked Pooh.

"Interjection. What we're doing now."

"Oh. Is that anything like an Interruption?"

"Well, something of the sort. I imagine."

Anyway, what we'd like to do in this Interruption is to explain that — we'll have to say this softly — this book isn't just about Pooh.

"Beg pardon?" said Pooh. "Did someone say something?"

"I didn't hear anything," said I.

"Oh," said Pooh.

"Er, Pooh — isn't that a rare bird in the tree outside the window? Or is it a fish?"

"I don't see anything in the tree," said Pooh.

"I'm sure it's a fish. One of the rare ones."

"It must be," said Pooh. "If it's up a tree."

"Do go and find out, won't you, Pooh? Here, I'll open the door for you. Take a good look. Good-bye."

* * *

Yes, this is not so much a *Pooh* book as it is a *Piglet*

book. In these pages, it will be the timid, yearning Piglet, rather than the comfortable, contented Pooh, who shows us the Way. In other words, we'll be looking at things from a slightly different angle. Since we are dealing with a more timid animal this time, this book may seem a bit more serious than its predecessor. But –

"Ah – there you are," said Rabbit. "Piglet's fallen into the wastebasket."

Perhaps *serious* isn't quite the word we want. Perhaps . . .

"*Help! Help!*"

. . . a better word would be *quieter*.

CRASH!!!***?
"What in heaven's name was that?"
"Tigger's rescued him," said Rabbit.
"Poor Piglet. Tell him I'll be there immediately."

Excuse me.

The – What Was That
Again? – of Piglet

One day when the sun had come back over
the Forest, bringing with it the scent of May,
and all the streams of the Forest were tinkling
happily to find themselves their own pretty
shape again, and the little pools lay dreaming of
the life they had seen and the big things they
had done, and in the warmth and quiet of the
Forest the cuckoo was trying over his voice
carefully and listening to see if he liked it, and
wood-pigeons were complaining gently to
themselves in their lazy comfortable way that it
was the other fellow's fault, but it didn't matter
very much; on such a day as this Christopher
Robin whistled in a special way he had, and
Owl came flying out of the Hundred Acre
Wood to see what was wanted.

"Ah — Pooh and Piglet. Come in and make yourselves comfortable. You're just in time."

"In time for what?" asked Pooh hopefully. "For a bit of — "

"For a bit of Taoism."

"Oh."

"Is it dangerous?" asked Piglet.

"Certainly not. You know what Taoism is."

"Yes," said Piglet, not quite sure. "Of course."

"You see, before we go any further, we need to explain Taoism."

"Didn't we do that already?" asked Pooh.

"That was in *The Tao of Pooh*. We need to say something Explanatory here, as well. Just in case."

"In case of what?" asked Piglet nervously.

"In case . . . Well, just in case. I suppose we could have Pooh say something about it, but he probably can't remember what it is."

"Of course I can," replied Pooh. "It's . . . That is, it's something like . . . Or is it? What I mean is . . ."

"That's what I thought."

"When you explained Taoism before," said Piglet, "you and Pooh went to China. If we do that, I'll need to pack some things."

"No, we won't be going to China. We're going to stay right here."

"That's good," said Pooh, wandering over to the kitchen.

"Because we'll begin with a Taoist explanation of the Origin of Taoism. And we might as well stay where we are, because wherever in the world we may be at any moment is where Taoism started — whether or not it was known there by that name. It began before the time of the Great Separation . . ."

Thousands of years ago, man lived in harmony with the rest of the natural world. Through what we would today call Telepathy, he communicated with animals, plants, and other forms of life — none of which he considered "beneath" himself, only different, with different jobs to perform. He worked side by side with earth angels and nature spirits, with whom he shared responsibility for taking care of the world.

The earth's atmosphere was very different from what it is now, with a great deal more vegetation-supporting moisture. A tremendous variety of vegetable, fruit, seed, and grain food was available. Because of such a diet, and a lack of unnatural strain, human life span was many times longer than what it is today. The killing of animals for food or "sport" was unthinkable. Man lived at peace with himself and the various life forms, whom he considered his teachers and friends.

But gradually at first, and then with increasing intensity, man's Ego began to grow and assert itself. Finally, after it had caused many unpleasant incidents, the consensus was reached that man should go out into the world alone, to learn a necessary lesson. The connections were broken.

On his own, feeling alienated from the world he had been created from, cut off from the full extent of its abundance, man was no longer happy. He began to search for the happiness he had lost. When he found something that reminded him of it, he tried to possess it and accumulate more – thereby introducing Stress into his life. But searching for lasting happiness and accumulating temporary substitutes for it brought him no satisfaction.

As he was no longer able to hear what the other forms of life were saying, he could only try to understand them through their actions, which he often misinterpreted. Because he was no longer cooperating with the earth angels and nature spirits for the good of all, but was attempting to manipulate the earth forces for his benefit alone, plants began to shrivel and die. With less vegetation to draw up and give off moisture, the planet's atmosphere became drier, and deserts appeared. A relatively small number of plant species survived, which grew smaller and tougher with passing time. Eventually they lost the radiant colors and abundant fruit of their ancestors. Man's life span began to shorten accordingly, and diseases appeared and spread. Because of the decreasing variety of food available to him — and his growing insensitivity — man began to kill and eat his friends the animals. They soon learned to flee from his approach and became increasingly shy and suspicious of human motives and behavior. And so the separation grew. After several generations, few people had any idea of what life had once been like.

As man became more and more manipulative of and violent toward the earth, and as his social and spiritual world narrowed to that of the human race alone, he became more and more manipulative of and violent toward his own kind. Men began to kill and enslave each other, creating armies and empires, forcing those who looked, talked, thought, and acted differently from them to submit to what they thought was best.

Life became so miserable for the human race that, around two to three thousand years ago, perfected spirits began to be born on earth in human form, to teach the truths that had largely been forgotten. But by then humanity had grown so divided, and so insensitive to the universal laws operating in the

natural world, that those truths were only partially
understood.

As time passed, the teachings of the perfected
spirits were changed, for what one might call political
reasons, by the all-too-human organizations that
inherited them. Those who came into prominence
within the organizations wanted power over others.
They downplayed the importance of non-human life
forms and eliminated from the teachings statements
claiming that those forms had souls, wisdom, and
divine presence – and that the heaven they were in
touch with was a state of Unity with the Divine that
could be attained by anyone who put aside his ego
and followed the universal laws. The power-hungry
wanted their followers to believe that heaven was a
place to which some people – and only people –
went after death, a place that could be reached by
those who had the approval of *their* organizations. So
not even the perfected spirits were able to restore
the wholeness of truth, because of interference by
the human ego.

Down through the centuries, accounts of the
Great Separation, and of the Golden Age that existed
before it, have been passed on by the sensitive and
wise. Today in the industrial West, they are classified
as mere legends and myths – fantasies believed in
by the credulous and unsophisticated, stories based

only on imagination and emotion. Despite the fact that quite a few people have seen and communicated with earth angels and nature spirits, and that more than one spiritual community has grown luscious fruits and vegetables by cooperating with them and following their instructions, descriptions of these beings are generally dismissed as "fairy tales." And, although colored and simplified accounts of the Great Separation can be found in the holy books of the world's religions, it is doubtful that many followers of those religions strongly believe in them.

However, a number of pre-Separation skills, beliefs, and practices have been preserved. On the North American continent, they are passed on in some of what remains of native teachings — those of the "Indians." In Europe they have largely died out, but traces of their influence can still be seen in such comparatively recent phenomena as stone circles and the marking of "ley lines" (called "dragon veins" by the Chinese) — channels along which earth energy is concentrated. In Tibet, until the Communist invasion, ancient ways were preserved in Tibetan Buddhism, many of the secrets and practices of which predate Buddhism by thousands of years. In Japan, they can be found in some of the rituals and beliefs of the Shinto ("spirit way") folk religion. In China, they have been passed on through Taoism. And, despite violent opposition from China's Communist government, they continue to be passed on today.

Briefly, Taoism is a way of living in harmony with *Tao*, the Way of the Universe, the character of which is revealed in the workings of the natural world. Taoism could be called either a philosophy or a religion, or neither, since in its various forms it does not match up with Western ideas or definitions of either one.

In China, Taoism is what might be called the counterbalance of Confucianism, the codified, ritualized teachings of K'ung Fu-tse, or "Master K'ung," better known in the West as Confucius. Although Confucianism is not a religion in the Western sense, it could be said to bear a certain resemblance to puritanical Christianity in its man-centered, nature-ignoring outlook, its emphasis on rigid conformity, and its authoritarian, No-Nonsense attitude toward life. Confucianism concerns itself mostly with human relations – with social and political rules and hierarchies. Its major contributions have been in the areas of government, business, clan and family relations, and ancestor reverence. Its most vital principles are Righteousness, Propriety, Benevolence, Loyalty, Good Faith, Duty, and Justice. Briefly stated, Confucianism deals with the individual's place within the group.

In contrast, Taoism deals primarily with the individual's relationship to the world. Taoism's contributions have been mostly scientific, artistic, and spiritual. From Taoism came Chinese science, medicine, gardening, landscape painting, and nature poetry. Its key principles are Natural Simplicity, Effortless Action, Spontaneity, and Compassion. The most easily noticed difference between Confucianism and Taoism is emotional, a difference in *feeling*: Confucianism is stern, regimented, patriarchal, often severe; Taoism is happy, gentle, childlike, and serene — like its favorite symbol, that of flowing water.

Taoism is classically viewed as the teachings of three men: Lao-tse ("Master Lao"), author of the major Taoist classic, the *Tao Tē Ching*, which is said to have been written around twenty-five hundred years ago; Chuang-tse ("Master Chuang"), author of several works and founder of a school of writers and philosophers during the Warring States period, approximately two thousand years ago; and the semilegendary Yellow Emperor, who ruled over forty-five hundred years ago, and to whom are attributed various meditative, alchemical, and medicinal principles and practices. These three were the great organizers and communicators of Taoist thought, rather than its founders; for, as we have said, what is now known as Taoism began before any of them were born, in what Chuangtse called the Age of Perfect Virtue:

> In the Age of Perfect Virtue, men lived among the animals and birds as members of one large family. There were no distinctions between "superior" and "inferior" to separate one man or species from another. All retained their natural Virtue and lived in the state of pure simplicity. . . .
>
> In the Age of Perfect Virtue, wisdom and ability were not singled out as extraordinary. The wise were seen merely as higher branches on humanity's tree, growing a little closer to the sun. People behaved correctly, without knowing that to be Righteousness and Propriety. They loved and respected each other, without calling that Benevolence. They were faithful and honest, without considering that to be Loyalty. They kept their word, without thinking of Good Faith. In their everyday conduct, they helped and employed each other, without considering Duty. They did not concern themselves with Justice, as there was no *injustice*. Living in harmony with themselves, each other, and the world, their actions left no trace, and so we have no physical record of their existence.★

★ This and other selections from classical oriental texts are my own translations and adaptations. – B.H.

Ever since the Great Separation, Taoists have concerned themselves with attaining the state of Perfect Virtue, through discarding whatever prevents harmony with Tao.

And with that mention of Virtue, we come to an explanation of the title of this book.

"I wondered when you were going to get around to that," said Piglet.

"So did I. But, anyway . . ."

First of all, we'd better explain that the Chinese character *Te*, as in "The *Te* of Piglet," is pronounced *DEH*, more or less. If you want to be particular, you can put a bit of an "r" sound at the end: *DEHr*. If you want to be even more particular, you can pronounce it halfway between *DEHr* and *DUHr*. And –

"And if you want to be more particular than *that*," interrupted Eeyore, "you can take a correspondence course."

"Oh – Eeyore. I didn't know you were here. I thought you were out in your swamp."

"Since we're being particular about things," said Eeyore, "it's a *bog* – B-O-G. Yes, I was there. Then I made the mistake of coming here. And now, having heard all I care to of this, I shall return."

"Well, don't let us detain you."

"So much for *explanations*," muttered Eeyore, on his way out the door.

"Eeyore's that way, isn't he?" said Piglet.

"Not all the time," I said. "Occasionally he's worse."

As we were saying, *Te* is pronounced *DEH*. In classical Chinese, it is written two ways. The first joins the character for "upright" to the character for "heart." Its meaning is *virtue*. The second way adds the character for "left foot," which in Chinese signifies "stepping out." Its meaning is *virtue in action*.

Te is not, as its English-language equivalent suggests, a one-size-fits-all sort of goodness or admired behavior that can be recognized as essentially the same no matter who possesses it. It is instead a quality of special character, spiritual strength, or hidden potential unique to the individual – something that comes from the Inner Nature of things. And something, we might add, that the individual who possesses it may be quite unaware of – as is the case with Piglet through most of the *Pooh* stories.

In this book, we are concerned with the transformation of Virtue into Virtue That Steps Out. And Piglet, we believe, is the *Pooh* animal best suited to demonstrate the process – because in the *Pooh* stories it is Piglet, and only Piglet, who undergoes just such a transformation.

Very Small Animal

The Piglet lived in a very grand house in the middle of a beech-tree, and the beech-tree was in the middle of the forest, and the Piglet lived in the middle of the house. Next to his house was a piece of broken board which had: "TRESPAS-SERS W" on it. When Christopher Robin asked the Piglet what it meant, he said it was his grandfather's name, and had been in the family for a long time. Christopher Robin said you *couldn't* be called Trespassers W, and Piglet said yes, you could, because his grandfather was, and it was short for Trespassers Will, which was short of Trespassers William. And his grandfather had had two names in case he lost one – Trespassers after an uncle, and William after Trespassers.

And so we are introduced to Piglet, in the third

chapter of *Winnie-the-Pooh*: Piglet, who craves security (he lives in the middle of a house in the middle of a tree in the middle of a forest); Piglet, who wants to be Somebody (so he invents a grandfather named Trespassers William); Piglet, a squeaky voice with pink cheeks; Piglet, the Very Small Animal. Unlike Pooh, who simply Is and Does, Piglet *Agonizes*.

For example, when Piglet and Pooh fell into the Gravel Pit . . .

> "Pooh," he went on nervously, and came a little closer, "do you think we're in a Trap?"
>
> Pooh hadn't thought about it at all, but now he nodded. For suddenly he remembered how he and Piglet had once made a Pooh Trap for Heffalumps, and he guessed what had happened. He and Piglet had fallen into a Heffalump Trap for Poohs! That was what it was.
>
> "What happens when the Heffalump comes?" asked Piglet tremblingly, when he had heard the news.
>
> "Perhaps he won't notice *you*, Piglet," said Pooh encouragingly, "because you're a Very Small Animal."
>
> "But he'll notice *you*, Pooh."
>
> "He'll notice *me*, and I shall notice *him*," said

Pooh, thinking it out. "We'll notice each other for a long time, and then he'll say: 'Ho-*ho*!' "

Piglet shivered a little at the thought of that "Ho-*ho*!" and his ears began to twitch.

"W-what will *you* say?" he asked.

Pooh tried to think of something he would say, but the more he thought, the more he felt that there *is* no real answer to "Ho-*ho*!" said by a Heffalump in the sort of voice this Heffalump was going to say it in.

"I shan't say anything," said Pooh at last. "I shall just hum to myself, as if I was waiting for something."

"Then perhaps he'll say, 'Ho-*ho*!' again?" suggested Piglet anxiously.

"He will," said Pooh.

Piglet's ears twitched so quickly that he had to lean them against the side of the Trap to keep them quiet.

"He will say it again," said Pooh, "and I shall go

on humming. And that will Upset him. Because
when you say 'Ho-*ho*!' twice, in a gloating sort
of way, and the other person only hums, you
suddenly find, just as you begin to say it the third
time – that – that – well, you find – "

What Pooh means to say is, it then isn't Ho-
ho-ish anymore. At least, that's what we *think* he means.

"But he'll say something else," said Piglet.

"That's just it. He'll say: 'What's all this?' And
then *I* shall say – and this is a very good idea,
Piglet, which I've just thought of – *I* shall say:
'It's a trap for a Heffalump which I've made, and
I'm waiting for the Heffalump to fall in.' And I
shall go on humming. That will Unsettle him."

"Pooh!" cried Piglet. . . . "You've saved us!"

"Have I?" said Pooh, not feeling quite sure.

But Piglet was quite sure; and his mind ran on,
and he saw Pooh and the Heffalump talking to
each other, and he thought suddenly, and a little
sadly, that it *would* have been rather nice if it had
been Piglet and the Heffalump talking so grandly
to each other, and not Pooh, much as he loved
Pooh; because he really had more brain than
Pooh, and the conversation would go better if
he and not Pooh were doing one side of it, and
it would be comforting afterwards in the evenings

to look back on the day when he answered a
Heffalump back as bravely as if the Heffalump
wasn't there. It seemed so easy now. He knew
just what he would say. . . .

And that's how it was in the Gravel Pit — until
Christopher Robin came along, looked down, and
saw Piglet and Pooh. Then things became a bit
Complicated:

"Ho-*ho!*" said Christopher Robin loudly and
suddenly.

Piglet jumped six inches in the air with Surprise
and Anxiety, but Pooh went on dreaming.

"It's the Heffalump!" thought Piglet nervously. "Now, then!" He hummed in his throat a little, so that none of the words should stick, and then, in the most delightfully easy way, he said: "Tra-la-la, tra-la-la . . ." But he didn't look round, because if you look round and see a Very Fierce Heffalump looking down at you, sometimes you forget what you were going to say.

"Rum-tum-tum-tiddle-um," said Christopher Robin in a voice like Pooh's . . .

"He's said the wrong thing," thought Piglet anxiously. "He ought to have said, 'Ho-*ho*!' again. Perhaps I had better say it for him." And, as fiercely as he could, Piglet said, "Ho-*ho*!"

"How *did* you get there, Piglet?" said Christopher Robin in his ordinary voice.

"This is Terrible," thought Piglet. "First he talks in Pooh's voice, and then he talks in Christopher Robin's voice, and he's doing it so as to Unsettle me." And being now Completely Unsettled, he said very quickly and squeakily: "This is a trap for Poohs, and I'm waiting to fall in it, ho-*ho*, what's all this, and then I say ho-*ho* again."

"*What?*" said Christopher Robin.

"A trap for ho-ho's," said Piglet huskily. "I've just made it, and I'm waiting for the ho-ho to come—come."

Not very impressive, we're afraid.

"Oh. Hello, Piglet. Who's that rough-looking man I've seen following you about lately?"

"He's my new Bodyguard," squeaked Piglet.

"*Bodyguard*? Why in the world do you need a *bodyguard*? Can't you look out for yourself?"

"I suppose so," replied Piglet. "But I feel so much more Secure this way."

"He looks pretty tough. I hope you checked his references."

"References?"

"Yes. From places he's worked before. Does he have a bad record – arrests, jail sentences, that sort of thing?"

"I – I don't *think* so," said Piglet.

"Well, I suppose it's all right. If you really think you need protection. By the way – what's happened to the old family silverware?"

"What?"

"You know – the silver knives, forks, spoons, and things. They're not in the drawer where they used to be. I just wondered if anything – "

"No," Piglet blurted out. "He couldn't have – I mean, they *couldn't* be. They've been misplaced or something. Yes, that's it. They *must* be. They . . . I . . . Excuse me, I must be going. Good-bye."

That's odd.

We might point out here that Taoism has always been fond of Very Small Animals. Aside from animals themselves – which Confucianists saw as mere things to eat, sacrifice, or pull plows and wagons – the Very Small Animals of traditional, Confucianist-dominated Chinese society were women, children, and the poor. Stepped on by greedy merchants, landholders, and government officials, the poor were at the very bottom of the Confucianist social scale. To put it another way, they weren't on it at all. Women, even those of wealthy families – *especially* those of wealthy families – weren't much better off, as the Confucianists practiced arranged marriage, polygamy, foot-binding (foot-*breaking*, actually), and other customs so repressive to women that no one in today's West could comprehend them. Children didn't have a very jolly time of it, either. To the staunch Confucianist, children existed to carry on the family line, unquestioningly obey their parents in every matter, and take every care of them in their old age – not to have ideas, ideals, and interests of their own. Under Confucianism, a father could justifiably kill a son who disobeyed or disgraced him, as such behavior was considered criminal.

In contrast, Taoism held that respect was something one earned, and that if Big Daddy misbehaved, his family had the right to rebel. That applied to the emperor and his "family" – his subjects – as well: If the emperor was a tyrant, the people had the right to take him off the throne. High Confucianist officials lived in constant fear of Taoist- and Buddhist-influenced secret societies that were ever ready to defend the stepped-on and attempt to topple the Dragon Throne if conditions became intolerable, which they often did.

Taoist sympathies were always with the Underdog – with the outcasts and unfortunates of Chinese society, including those financially ruined by the tricks of corrupt merchants and officials and forced to become "Brothers of the Green Woods" (outlaws) and "Guests of Rivers and Lakes" (vagabonds). The Chinese martial arts were developed primarily by Taoists and Buddhist monks, in order to defend the defenseless and enable them to defend themselves. They might better be termed the *anti*-martial arts, as they were employed not only against armed bandits, but also against the soldiers of warlords and governing bodies, whenever they turned their swords against the weak. While Buddhist martial artists tended to concentrate on the "hard" forms of defense (from which evolved the forceful and direct *Karate* and *Tae Kwon Do*), Taoists tended to concentrate on the "soft" forms, such as the fluid and indirect *T'ai Chi Ch'üan* and *Pa Kua Chang* (similar to, but more sophisticated than, *Judo* and *Aikido*).

In countering what they saw as abuse of power, Taoist writers did with their communicative skills what Taoist martial artists did with disarming moves and pressure points. Utilizing the vehicles of literary fact and fiction, they publicized the misdeeds of the powerful and ridiculed the devious, the arrogant, the pompous, and the cruel. Although annoyed Confucianists often attempted to put an end to these writings, they were generally unsuccessful, as the sympathies of the common people were against them.

Considering that High and Mighty Confucianists tended to have little respect for animals, and that they sometimes referred to the "lesser" peoples of China as "pigs" and "dogs," it is not surprising that Taoist writers recorded many animal stories – descriptions of actual occurrences as well as imaginary tales – in which maligned creatures such as mice, snakes, and birds of prey demonstrate virtuous conduct that Prestigious People would do well to emulate. In these stories, the courage, affection, faithfulness, and honesty of animals are contrasted with the pretentiousness and hypocrisy of wealthy landholders, merchants, and government officials. As an early example, Chuang-tse wrote:

The Officer of Prayer went to the pigpen in his official robes, and spoke to the pigs. "Why should you complain?" he asked. "I will feed you grain for three months. Then I will fast for ten days – while you eat – and keep watch over you for three days after that. Then I will spread fresh mats and place you on the carved sacrificial stand, before dispatching you to the spirit world. Considering all that I will be doing for you, why should you feel uneasy?"

If the official had been truly concerned with the welfare of the pigs, he would have fed them bran and chaff and left them alone. But he looked at the situation from the point of view of his own prestige. He preferred to enjoy the robes and cap of his privileged office, and to ride about in an ornamented carriage – knowing that when *he* died, he would be carried in splendor to his grave, a magnificent canopy spread above his coffin. If he had been concerned with the welfare of the pigs, he would not have considered these things to be important.

Wealthy Confucianists weren't the only targets of Taoist writers. Like the Marx Brothers or Stan Laurel and Oliver Hardy, the Taoists satirized Big Ego at any level of society. This tendency can be seen in the following story, "The Pear Seed," by the Ch'ing Dynasty writer P'u Sung-ling:

A well-dressed farmer was selling his pears in
the town marketplace. As they were large and
delicious, he was soon taking in quite a bit of
money. A passing Taoist, dressed in patched cotton
and carrying a small shovel on his back, stopped
by the farmer's wagon and asked for a pear. The
farmer's told him to go away. The Taoist refused
to leave. The farmer grew angrier and angrier.
Soon he was shouting at the top of his voice.

"But there are hundreds of pears in your wagon,"
the Taoist calmly pointed out. "I'm only asking
for one. Why be so upset?"

More and more people gathered, attracted by the
commotion. Some onlookers told the farmer to
toss the poor man a bruised pear. The farmer
refused. Finally, seeing that the uproar was about
to turn into a riot, someone bought a pear and
handed it to the Taoist. After warmly thanking
his benefactor, the Taoist turned to the crowd.

"We followers of the Way are revolted by petty
greed," he told them. "Let me share this beautiful
fruit with you kind people."

No one wanted to take a piece of the Taoist's
pear. The spectators insisted that he eat it himself.

"All I need is a seed to plant," the Taoist replied,
"and then I'll be able to repay you." He ate the
fruit, except for one small seed. With his little
shovel he dug a hole, dropped the seed into it,

and covered it over. Then he called for heated water. Someone brought some from a nearby shop. The crowd watched in intense fascination as the Taoist watered the ground where the seed was planted.

Suddenly a small shoot appeared, which quickly grew into a tree. Branches and leaves shot out in great profusion. The tree blossomed, then bore a tremendous crop of large, luscious pears.

The Taoist distributed the fruit among the spectators. Soon all of it was gone. Then, with his small shovel, he chopped down the tree. Waving to the crowd, he happily departed, dragging the tree behind him.

All this time, the greedy farmer had been staring, openmouthed. Now he turned back to his pears – only to find that they were gone. Shaking off the effects of the Taoist's spell, he realized what had happened to them. He saw that a section of his wagon's harnessing pole – the same diameter as the trunk of the "pear tree" – had been chopped away.

After a frantic search, the farmer found the pole leaning against a wall, where the Taoist had left it. As for the Taoist, he was nowhere to be seen. The crowd roared with laughter in appreciation of the instructive joke.

Did someone just come in? Oh.

"So you're Piglet's new bodyguard. Well, well."
"You got a *problem* with that, buddy?"
"No, not at all."
"Good. I wouldn't get any *ideas* if I was you, fella."
"Oh, yes you would. You'd get all sorts of ideas.
Such as how easy it is to pull someone off his feet
with a loose rug – like the one you're standing on."
"What're you *talkin'* about?"
"Oh, nothing. Just make yourself at home."
"T'anks."

In order to understand Taoist support of the
Underdog, one needs to understand the Taoist attitude
toward power, from the Power of the Universe on
down. As with other matters, the Taoist view
was historically more or less the opposite of the
Confucianist.

The Confucianist conception of Heavenly Power,
vague though it tended to be, bore a certain resemblance to the Middle Eastern, Old Testament image
of God. The Confucianists called it *T'ien* – "Sky,"
"Heaven," or "Supreme Ruler." T'ien was seen as
masculine, sometimes ferociously so. It needed to be
appeased with sacrifices and rituals. It took sides; it
granted authority. It transmitted sovereignty directly

to the emperor, the Son of Heaven. From him, dominion spread downward and outward – from the highest officials to the lowest, from the major clans to the minor families. T'ien was imagined as dazzling in appearance (hence the brilliant colors used by the imperial family and the great clans). It was said to grant material prosperity as a reward (hence the Confucianist equation of wealth with goodness). In a word, it was considered *awesome* – something to fear, rather than love (hence the emphasis on unquestioning obedience to superiors, and the absence of words such as *compassion* from the Confucianist vocabulary). Such was the image of Heavenly Power that Confucianists presented to the common people. At the community level, it was shown in the courtroom treatment of complainants, witnesses, and the accused, not one of whom was allowed legal counsel or defense: All had to kneel on a hard floor (sometimes on chains) before the magistrate, who, as the emperor's representative in local government, had the right to extract testimony and confessions by torture – and, since under Chinese law no criminal could be sentenced until he had confessed, torture was the order of the day (hence the development of Chinese Torture). Because of centuries of this sort of intimidation, the majority of Chinese have tended to avoid whenever possible the workings of official government.

Unfortunately, this Unwillingness to Openly Participate has allowed one tyrant after another — including those of the present totalitarian bureaucracy — to gain and maintain control of the nation.

Unlike the Confucianists, Taoists saw the Power of Heaven as both masculine and feminine, as symbolized by the Taoist *T'ai Chi* — the circle divided by a curved line into light and dark, or male and female, halves. Heavenly Power at work in the natural world, however — what Lao-tse called "The Mother of Ten Thousand Things" — has always been seen by Taoists as mostly feminine in its actions. It is gentle, like flowing water. It is humble and generous, like a fertile valley, feeding all who come to it. It is hidden, subtle, and mysterious, like a landscape glimpsed through mist. It takes no sides, grants no authority. It cannot be influenced or appeased by sacrifices and rituals. In dispensing justice, as in all things, it operates with a light touch, an invisible hand. As Lao-tse put it, "Heaven's net has wide meshes, but nothing slips through." Shying away from displays of arrogance and egotism, it communicates its deepest secrets not to high government officials, pompous scholars, or wealthy landowners, but to penniless monks, little children, animals, and "fools." If it can be said to be biased in any way, it is in favor of the humble, the weak, the small.

And that brings us back to Piglet.

As anyone can see, there are disadvantages to being a Very Small Animal. And one of those disadvantages is that bigger animals will try to take advantage of you. For example, let's recall Rabbit's famous Plan to Kidnap Baby Roo.

Practically as soon as Kanga and Roo arrived in the Forest, Rabbit decided that they ought to leave. We're not sure why – Rabbits are like that, sometimes. Anyway, Rabbit's plan involved – which in Rabbit terminology means *took advantage of* – Piglet and Pooh.

The idea was, Pooh would distract Kanga by talking to her, perhaps reciting some of his poetry (which ought to distract anyone). And – Ouch!

"That was uncalled for, Pooh."

"Was it?" asked Pooh. "I thought I heard you calling it."

And while Kanga's attention was diverted, Rabbit would place Piglet in her pouch – telling her it was Roo – and then run off with Roo. Afterward, when Kanga had discovered that Roo was missing . . . Then Rabbit, Pooh, and Piglet – all three of them, mind you – would say "*Aha!*" very loudly. As Rabbit explained it, a loud "*Aha!*" would mean that they had kidnapped Roo and would give him back only if

Kanga were to promise to leave the Forest and never return. Kanga would grasp this meaning immediately, Rabbit said, as soon as Rabbit, Pooh, and Piglet (all three, mind you) said "*Aha!*" It went wrong – as Clever Plans by Rabbit always do – because first, Kangas think and respond differently from Rabbits; and second, as things turned out there was no loud, group-spoken "*Aha!*" to intimidate her, whether or not she would have understood what it was supposed to mean, anyway.

The first part of the plan went smoothly enough. They came across Kanga and Roo in the forest. Pooh distracted Kanga, Piglet jumped into Kanga's pouch, and Rabbit ran off with Roo. Unsuspecting Kanga bounced home with (bounce, bounce) Piglet (bounce, bounce, bounce). Pooh remained behind, practicing (thud) Kanga-jumps (crash). It wasn't until Kanga reached her house that the Trouble began:

> Of course as soon as Kanga unbuttoned her pocket, she saw what had happened. Just for a moment, she thought she was frightened, and then she knew she wasn't; for she felt quite sure that Christopher Robin would never let any harm happen to Roo. So she said to herself, "If they are having a joke with me, I will have a joke with them."

"Now then, Roo, dear," she said as she took Piglet out of her pocket. "Bed-time."

"*Aha!*" said Piglet, as well as he could after his Terrifying Journey. But it wasn't a very good "*Aha!*" and Kanga didn't seem to understand what it meant.

"Bath first," said Kanga in a cheerful voice.

"*Aha!*" said Piglet again, looking round anxiously for the others. But the others weren't there . . .

"I am not at all sure," said Kanga in a thoughtful voice, "that it wouldn't be a good idea to have a *cold* bath this evening. Would you like that, Roo, dear?"

Whether Roo would have or not, *Piglet* didn't.
But at last, the Cold Bath was over . . .

"Now," said Kanga, "there's your medicine, and
then bed."

"W-w-what medicine?" said Piglet.

"To make you grow big and strong, dear. You
don't want to grow up small and weak like Piglet,
do you? Well, then!"

At that moment there was a knock at the door.

"Come in," said Kanga, and in came Christopher
Robin.

"Christopher Robin, Christopher Robin!" cried
Piglet. "Tell Kanga who I am! She keeps saying
I'm Roo. I'm *not* Roo, am I?"

Christopher Robin looked at him very carefully, and shook his head.

"You can't be Roo," he said, because I've just seen Roo playing in Rabbit's house."

"Well!" said Kanga. "Fancy that! Fancy my making a mistake like that."

"There you are!" said Piglet. "I told you so. I'm Piglet."

Christopher Robin shook his head again.

"Oh, you're not Piglet," he said. "I know Piglet well, and he's *quite* a different color."

Piglet began to say that this was because he had just had a bath, and then he thought that perhaps he wouldn't say that, and as he opened his mouth to say something else, Kanga slipped the medicine spoon in, and then patted him on the back and told him that it was really quite a nice taste when you got used to it.

What an ordeal. Well, that's what happens.

"*Hey! What's dat noise outside?*"

"Oh. Piglet's bodyguard. I'd forgotten you were here. It's some sort of siren, I think. Let me take a look . . . Yes – it's a police car."

"*What?*"

"That's strange. It's pulling up right in front of our house."

"*Get away from dat window!*"

"Of course. I didn't mean to –" Where'd he go?

Excuse me. I have to answer the door.

Little Piglet – held back by imaginings and fears, yearning to be Someone – is the last animal one might expect to accomplish anything of importance. And yet Piglet is the material from which heroes are made. Beneath the stalwart exterior of most any Courageous Rescuer, Gallant Fighter, or Great Achiever, a Piglet can be found, if one looks closely enough. So it has always been, as history clearly shows; and so, we're sure, it will always be.

In many ways, Piglet may appear the least

significant of the *Pooh* characters. Yet he is the only one of them to change, to grow, to become more than what he was in the first place. And in the end, he does this not by denying his smallness, but by applying it, for the good of others. He accomplishes what he does without accumulating a Large Ego; inside, he remains a Very Small Animal – but a different *kind* of Very Small Animal from what he was before.

For now, though, he hesitates and dreams. He has a good deal to go through before the Great Storm at the end of *The House at Pooh Corner*, which changes his life forever.

"How would *you* sum up Piglet's situation at this point, Pooh?"

"With a song," said Pooh.

"Wonderful. I was hoping you would."

"(er*hum*) . . ."

Animal so shy and small,
Dreaming you were Bold and Tall –
You hesitate, all sensitive,
Waiting for a chance to Live.

Time is swift, it races by;
Opportunities are born and die . . .
Still you wait and will not try –

A bird with wings who dares not
* rise and fly.*

But that You you want to see
Is not you, and will never be.
No one else will ever do
The special things that wait
* inside of you.*

You can be a guiding star,
If you make the most of Who You Are.
And the sensitivity
That you're now ashamed to see
Can be developed even more,
So you can find the hidden doors
To places no one's been before.
And the pride you'll feel inside
Is not the kind that makes you fall —
It's the kind that recognizes
The bigness found in being Small.

"Thank you, Pooh. That was excellent."

"Well," said Pooh, "it was better than I'd thought it would be."

Along the way to developing and applying Sensitivity, there are things a Piglet needs to watch out for. And one of them is found in the next chapter.

The Eeyore Effect

"What's the matter, Piglet?" I asked.

"I was walking through the flowers just now," he said, "singing a little song, when Eeyore came up."

"Oh. Eeyore. What happened?"

"He said, 'Be careful, little Piglet – someone might pick you along with those pansies and put you in a vase on the mantelpiece. And *then* what would you do?' Then he walked away, chuckling to himself."

"Oh, don't mind Eeyore. He just likes to make others feel small, especially if they're smaller than he is, anyway. That makes him look big – he thinks."

"I wouldn't mind his being miserable by himself, if he enjoys it so. But why does he have to spread it around?"

There is something in each of us that wants us to be Unhappy. It creates in our imaginations problems that don't yet exist – quite often causing them to come true. It exaggerates problems that are already there. It reinforces low self-esteem and lack of respect for others. It destroys pride in workmanship, order, and cleanliness. It turns meetings into Confrontations, expectations into Dread, opportunities into Danger, stepping stones into Stumbling Blocks. It can be seen at work in grimaces and frowns, which pull the muscles of the face forward and down, speeding the aging process. It contaminates the mind behind the face with its negative energy and spreads outward, like a disease. And then it comes back, projected and reflected by other unhappy minds and faces. And on it goes.

Norman Cousins, editor of the *Saturday Review* for over thirty years, described the Eeyore Effect in an article he wrote following that magazine's demise:

> Whatever success the *Saturday Review* may have had was directly connected to its respect for the place of ideas and the arts in the life of the mind. This emphasis takes on special significance in the light of the sleaziness that has infected the national culture in recent years. There seems to be a fierce competition, especially in

entertainment and publishing, to find ever-lower rungs on the ladder of taste . . .

There is the curious notion that freedom is somehow synonymous with gutter jargon. At one time people who worked in the arts would boast to one another about their ability to communicate ideas that attacked social injustice and brutality. Now some of them seem to feel that they have struck a blow for humanity if only they can use enough four-letter words . . .

The debasement of language not only reflects but produces a retreat from civility. The slightest disagreement has become an occasion for violent reactions. Television has educated an entire generation of Americans to believe that the normal way of reacting to a slight is by punching someone in the face.

The Eeyore Effect can be seen in every socially accepted negative phenomenon, such as the growing number of elderly young people whose governing philosophy seems to be: It Won't Work, So Why Try? Or in today's Death Camp Chic fashions, and the popular Ugly-Skinny-Angry Look:

"Lobelia is dressed to kill or be killed in this stunning black leather ensemble positively glowing with terrorist charm. It's the look, the appeal, the special touch that says Harley-Davidson. *Put away that knife, Lobelia!* For heaven's sake! Somebody, please – take it from her before she causes some real harm."

The original Eeyore had at least a certain grim sense of humor, a sort of funnyness-with-its-lights-turned-out. Latter-day Eeyores seem to be missing that. One thing they *do* have, however, is fear. Eeyores are afraid – afraid to risk positive emotional expression, positive action, positive involvement in anything beyond Ego. Those things are stupid, they say, and they don't want to look stupid. (They don't seem to mind looking Paralyzed with Fear – they just don't want to look *stupid*.) Unfortunately for those around them, complaining is one thing that Eeyores are not afraid to do. They grudgingly carry their thimbles to the Fountain of Life, then mumble and grumble that they weren't given enough.

"Hallo, Eeyore," said Christopher Robin, as he opened the door and came out. "How are *you?*"

"It's snowing still," said Eeyore gloomily.

"So it is."

"*And* freezing."

"Is it?"

"Yes," said Eeyore. "However," he said, brightening up a little, "we haven't had an earthquake lately."

Eeyores are Realists, they say. But reality is what one makes it. And the more negative reality one nurtures and creates, the more of it one has. Eeyores see only what they want to . . . For example, never before in history has the individual had so much power, and so many opportunities to effect change. That assertion can be easily verified by taking a good look around. But the Eeyore Effect makes a great many people believe that they are powerless. And because they *believe* they're powerless, they are.

"I don't know how it is, Christopher Robin, but
what with all this snow and one thing and
another, not to mention icicles and such-like, it
isn't so Hot in my field about three o'clock in
the morning . . ."

Without difficulties, life would be like a stream
without rocks and curves – about as interesting as
concrete. Without problems, there can be no personal
growth, no group achievement, no progress for
humanity. But what matters about problems is what
one *does* with them. Eeyores don't overcome problems.
No, it's the other way around.

"And I said to myself: The others will be sorry if I'm getting myself all cold. They haven't got Brains, any of them, only grey fluff that's blown into their heads by mistake, and they don't Think, but if it goes on snowing for another six weeks or so, one of them will begin to say to himself: 'Eeyore can't be so very much too Hot about three o'clock in the morning.' And then it will Get About. And they'll be Sorry."

Eeyores, in other words, are Whiners. They believe the negative but not the positive and are so obsessed with What's Wrong that the Good Things in Life pass them by unnoticed. Are they the ones, then, to give us an accurate account of what life is about? If the universe were governed by the Eeyore Attitude, the whole thing would have collapsed eons ago. Everything in creation, from migrating hummingbirds to

spinning planets, operates on the belief that It Can
Be Done. To quote William Blake, "If the Sun and
Moon should Doubt/They'd immediately Go Out."

Therefore, no society that wants to last is going
to be guided by Eeyores. For Eeyores sneer at the
very things that are needed most for survival and
prosperity. As Lao-tse wrote:

> *When they hear of the Way,*
> *The highest minds practice it;*
> *The average minds think about it*
> *And try it now and then;*
> *The lowest minds laugh at it.*
> *If they did not laugh at it,*
> *It would not be the Way.*

Pardon me a moment. This letter just arrived.

"Fan mail for Pooh, I suppose," said Piglet enviously.
"For me?" said Pooh, waking up suddenly.
"No, it's . . . Hmm. I'll read it to you."

> "Dear Sir:
> "It has come to my attention that in your trifling
> book, *The Tao of Pooh,* you fail to mention a single
> positive attribute of that most charming of the
> A. A. Milne characters. I refer, of course, to the
> loveable ~~EOR~~ Eeyore.

"It is beyond my understanding how anyone
could overlook the merits of the affable, debonair,
and instigorating ~~EOR~~ Eeyore. His wit and
wisdom can serve as an example to all in these
dark days that envelop us."

"Dark?" said Pooh, looking out the window.
"Where?"

"That's just a figure of speech, Pooh."

"Oh. One of those."

"He must have been in the dark when he *wrote*
it," said Piglet, studying the letter.

"Do you mean the writing? It is pretty awful. But
to continue . . ."

"Yes, in these times of tedium and ineptitude, it
is refreshing — and encouraging — to know that
there exists such a valuable, admirable, and *humble*
animal as ~~EOR~~ Eeyore.

A Friend"

"P.S. Don't do it again."

Well, now we've heard from — er, whoever it was
who sent this letter. I have a feeling that we'll hear
from him again.

Let's look at some Eeyores Around Us. We will
begin with what we call the Negative News Media.

As Henry David Thoreau wrote, in *Walden*:

> I am sure that I never read any memorable news
> in a newspaper. If we read of one man robbed,
> or murdered, or killed by accident, or one house
> burned, or one vessel wrecked, or one steamboat
> blown up, or one cow run over on the Western
> Railroad, or one mad dog killed, or one lot of
> grasshoppers in the winter – we never need read
> of another. One is enough.

Today, thanks to the Negative News Media, we
are overinformed about problems we can do little or
nothing about. Despite the great fanfare made about
these problems, few of them have much of anything
to do with our lives. When it comes to those that *do*
– such as the matter of what the local Nuclear Power
Plant is doing to our health – the media are quite
often silent. Strange. The Negative News Media rarely
tell us of problems we can do something about, and
never tell us what we can do about them. That would
give us an unfair advantage, we suppose.

The Negative News Media sneer at everything
and everyone, and call that Objectivity. Although there
are courageous, noble-minded investigators and
communicators in the news business, all too many of
the rest behave like Peeping Toms with notebooks
and cameras, who seem more interested in destroying

heroes than in exposing villains. If the media build up some individuals in the public eye, it seems to be for the purpose of rubbing their remains in the public eye later on, in order to sell automobiles and tooth-paste.

The heroes have flaws, we're told. Like Tigger, they can climb up but not down; their tails get in the way. So-and-So is just an ordinary man, after all. (That's a crime?) Such-and-Such is a crook. For some reason, however, the negative newsmongers tend to ignore the doings of the Biggest Crooks in the Highest Places – the ones who cause the greatest damage. Last month's Admirable People are now in disgrace and will quickly fade from sight. A new set will pop up in the latest broadcast or magazine issue, like targets in a shooting gallery. They in turn will be gunned down, and so on. The engineering of this process reminds us of some other words of William Blake: "A Truth that's told with bad intent/Beats all the Lies you can invent."

In reality, heroes are heroic because they, despite their weaknesses – and sometimes *because of* them – do great things. If they were perfect, they wouldn't be here in earth's classroom. Their strengths and weaknesses *could* be presented in an objective manner, for the enlightenment of others. But that's not what the Negative News Media do. Instead, they focus on the flaws in the most sensational manner, in order to make themselves wealthy. Who is going to take a chance at doing anything more than the mediocre, and help others to do the same, knowing that the Negative News Media are awaiting an opportunity to bring him crashing to the ground before an audience of millions?

Just as important, what effect does this constant character assassination have on that audience itself? To quote further from Henry David Thoreau . . .

> If I am to be a thoroughfare, I prefer that it be of the mountain brooks, the Parnassian streams, and not the town sewers. There is inspiration, that gossip which comes to the ear of the attentive mind from the courts of heaven. There is the profane and stale revelation of the barroom and the police court. The same ear is fitted to receive both communications. . . . We should treat our minds, that is, ourselves, as innocent and in- genuous children, whose guardians we are, and be careful what objects and what subjects we thrust on their attention. Read not the *Times*. Read the Eternities.

Oops. Here he comes.

"Has anybody heard the news?" asked Eeyore,

walking gloomily into the room.

"What is it now?" said I.

"Disaster. Horrendous, unspeakable *disaster*."

"I thought that was yesterday. Or the day before."

"It's in all the papers," said Eeyore, ignoring me as best he could.

"At what time does the earth explode?" I inquired, turning to look at the clock.

"Very amusing," said Eeyore. "In a pathetic sort of way."

"And when," I asked, "is the sun going dead?"

"Ha, ha. It's just what you *would* say. The sun going dead. Only don't blame me if it doesn't."

"All right, I won't. But I might blame you if it *does*."

All this about newspapers, gossip, and such brings us to those classic Eeyore killjoys and spoil-sports known as The Critics. You know what they are, whether they be professional Reputation Smashers or the Old Grump next door. If you sing, they can sing better (even though they can't sing). If you dance, they can dance better (even though they can't dance). If you direct a theater production, they can direct better (even though they can't direct). Whatever you do, they can do it better, even though they can't do it as well as you can. And since they can't *do* it as well as you, it shouldn't be particularly surprising if they don't accurately *judge* it. Whether in condemning Works of Genius or in praising the Truly Awful, The Critics tend to be wrong a disturbingly large amount of the time. Yet they can have tremendous influence, just the same. And that influence is responsible for the tragic loss of much that would have been of benefit to the world.

Chuang-tse described the limitations of The Critics in his story about a know-it-all quail:

> There is a great bird known as the P'eng. Its back appears as broad as a mountain range; its wings are like clouds across the sky. It rises up like a whirlwind until it breaks through the high mist and soars into the infinite blue.
>
> As it glides effortlessly along on its journey to the sea, a quail in the marsh looks up at it and laughs. "What does that bird think it's doing?" says the quail. "I jump up and fly a few feet; then I come down and flutter from here to there in the bushes. *That* is what flying is for! Who is that creature trying to fool?"
>
> . . . So it is that the knowledge of the small-minded cannot reach to that which is great, just as the experience of a few years cannot equal that of many. The mushroom of a morning knows not what takes place at the end of the month;

the short-lived cicada has no awareness of what
happens in the seasons beyond.

Our favorite story about The Critics was told to
us a few years ago by someone-or-other, who'd heard
it who-knows-where:

> While traveling separately through the country-
> side late one afternoon, a Hindu, a Rabbi, and a
> Critic were caught in the same area by a terrific
> thunderstorm. They sought shelter at a nearby
> farmhouse.
>
> "That storm will be raging for hours," the farmer
> told them. "You'd better stay here for the night.
> The problem is, there's only room enough for
> two of you. One of you'll have to sleep in the
> barn."
>
> "I'll be the one," said the Hindu. "A little hardship
> is nothing to me." He went out to the barn.
>
> A few minutes later, there was a knock at the
> door. It was the Hindu. "I'm sorry," he told the
> others, "but there is a cow in the barn. According
> to my religion, cows are sacred, and one must
> not intrude into their space."
>
> "Don't worry," said the Rabbi. "Make yourself
> comfortable here. I'll go to sleep in the barn."
> He went out to the barn.

A few minutes later, there was a knock at the door. It was the Rabbi. "I hate to be a bother," he said, "but there is a pig in the barn. In my religion, pigs are considered unclean. I wouldn't feel comfortable sharing my sleeping quarters with a pig."

"Oh, all right," said the Critic. "*I'll* go sleep in the barn." He went out to the barn.

A few minutes later, there was a knock at the door. It was the cow and the pig.

The Critics can be pretty intimidating, all right. One can't do or say much of anything without fear of offending this particular — *very* particular — type of Eeyore. If you do or say the wrong thing (or the right thing), you may find yourself ostracized. But being Ostracized by Eeyores has its advantages. At least you don't have to associate with —

"Ostrich-sized?" said Pooh. "How can you be ostrich-sized? Unless you're an ostrich."

"No, not ostrich-sized. Ostracized."

"That's rather large, isn't it?" said Piglet. "They're such very big birds."

"No — not *ostrich*-sized. *Ostracized*."

"They *are* big birds," said Owl.

"Now look here, all of you — "

"In fact, the male of the genus *Struthio* can attain a height of eight feet and a weight of three hundred pounds. As one might imagine, they can be quite dangerous when angered, and — "

Excuse me while I take this material into another room.

> It was the first party to which Roo had ever been, and he was very excited. As soon as ever they had sat down he began to talk.
>
> "Hallo, Pooh!" he squeaked.
>
> "Hallo, Roo!" said Pooh.
>
> Roo jumped up and down in his seat for a little while and then began again.
>
> "Hallo, Piglet!" he squeaked.
>
> Piglet waved a paw at him, being too busy to say anything.
>
> "Hallo, Eeyore!" said Roo.
>
> Eeyore nodded gloomily at him. "It will rain soon, you see if it doesn't."

Next we come to the Educator Eeyores, whose idea of teaching is *impress the maximum number of Unpleasant Things upon children at the minimum possible age*. Perhaps in the past these Eeyores were stepped on once too often by the Heel of Fortune and now want to take out their frustrations on people smaller than they are. Perhaps they truly believe that their approach to teaching is the best (despite the fact that few of their graduating students can even spell, or punctuate a sentence). We don't know. But we do know that their approach to education works against natural laws at practically every step of the way.

Mentally, emotionally, and physically, the human being is designed for a long childhood, followed by a short adolescence and then adulthood – the state of responsible, self-reliant wholeness. What we see children experiencing now, however, is an ever-shorter childhood, followed by a premature, prolonged adolescence from which ever fewer seem to be emerging.

Rather than help children develop the abilities needed to overcome the difficulties immediately confronting them, in the natural order in which they need to develop them, the Eeyore Educational System (with a good deal of help from parents and the entertainment industry) is forcing too much inappropriate information on them too soon, concerning – and causing – problems they can do nothing about. Then the children get stuck.

In response to the declining Test Scores of recent

years, the educational system has brought in vastly expensive *machines* to do the teaching – a sign of trouble if there ever was one. Learn to write from a computer, and so on. (Of course, it *could* have brought in people who knew how to write, or whatever, to teach how to write, or whatever – on a volunteer basis, if necessary. But that would have been too simple, we suppose. Cheating, almost.) Now this costly Teaching Technology is bankrupting the system. So, in order to Cut Costs, the Eeyores are eliminating what *they* consider unnecessary classes – Art, Creative Writing, Drama, and so on – classes that help students observe, reason, and communicate, as well as keep their spirits and the right sides of their brains alive.

The Eeyore Educational System sees childhood as a waste of time, a luxury that society cannot afford. Its response to the problems of vanishing childhood is to speed up the process – give the students more information, give it to them at a faster rate, and give it to them sooner. Put children in school at the earliest age possible; load them down with homework; take away their time, their creativity, their play, their power; then plug them into machines. That'll whip them into shape. Well, it'll whip them, anyway.

Over two thousand years ago, Chuang-tse described a similar situation:

The ancient emperor Shun encouraged rivalry in the minds of the people. Children were born the usual number of months after conception; but five months after that, they were being taught to converse. Soon they were calling people by their titles and personal names. Then men began to die while still young. . . .

This governing provided order in name only. In reality, it produced chaos. It ran contrary to the light of the sun and the moon, brought harm to the mountains and rivers, and poisoned the fruit of the four seasons. It proved more deadly than the sting of a scorpion, or the bite of a dangerous beast.

The more that children are Educated by Eeyores, the more problems they develop. And the more problems they develop, the more the Eeyores insist on Educating them, at an ever-earlier age. The Educator Eeyores' answer to the problems that the Eeyores create is: Crack Down. The children's response is: Crack Up.

Piglet had got up early that morning to pick himself a bunch of violets; and when he had picked them and put them in a pot in the middle of his house, it suddenly came over him that nobody had ever picked Eeyore a bunch of violets, and the more he thought of this, the more he thought how sad it was to be an Animal who had never had a bunch of violets picked for him. So he hurried out again, saying to himself, "Eeyore, Violets," and then "Violets, Eeyore," in case he forgot, because it was that sort of day, and he picked a large bunch and trotted along, smelling them, and feeling very happy, until he came to the place where Eeyore was.

"Oh, Eeyore," began Piglet a little nervously, because Eeyore was busy.

Eeyore put out a paw and waved him away.

"Tomorrow," said Eeyore. "Or the next day."

Like the Iron Fist educators just mentioned, the following Eeyores work against natural laws and then complain about the results. In their behavior, they might be said to personify the opposite of the Taoist belief that the masculine and feminine earth energies need to be kept in balance, and that when the masculine is excessive the feminine needs to be advanced.

The rather Severe people we're thinking of might be called the Eeyore Amazons. They are emotionally descended from the Puritans – those grim souls who considered femininity No Good, along with art, music, dancing, singing, the natural world, and practically everything else that makes life enjoyable. As do a number of other people (us included), the Eeyore Amazons call themselves feminists. But the word doesn't quite fit them, somehow. They don't like femininity. Instead, they covet masculinity. Strange. Very strange.

Rather like certain joggers who are so automobile-oriented that they run on asphalt highways, gulping down noxious gases with every breath, the Eeyore Amazons are so masculinity-oriented that they think of success, power, and all that in aggressive, combative masculine terms.

And so, just when a good many of us men have discarded earth-family-and-society-damaging *machismo*, along come the Eeyore Amazons, cursing and plundering like pirates in a bad Hollywood movie. Not exactly what we would call Advancing the Feminine. Yet even as they imitate and increase the worst sort of masculine energy, they denounce practically everything they dislike as masculine and a threat – to the extent of seeing masculinity and threats that aren't there. Stranger and stranger.

For example, the Amazons want to eliminate what they call the "masculine" (neutral) nouns, pronouns, and adjectives of the English language because, they say, these words are demeaning to women. Then they substitute words that are demeaning to everyone.

First, they made us change *chairman* to *chairperson* – which meant the same thing as *chairman*, only it was harder to say, longer to write, and just a bit silly. After a while, recognizing that *chairperson* was indeed rather awkward and stupid, they made us change it to *chair*. You know what a chair is. It's a thing. You sit on it.

So now Plain English has been turned into patronizing Lawyer-Politicianese . . .

> If a person does not keep pace with his or her companions, perhaps it is because he or she hears a different drummer [or drummerette?]. Let him, or her, step to the music which he, or she, hears, however measured or far away.

. . . and equally nonsensical Pluralspeak:

> If a person does not keep pace with their companions, perhaps it is because they hear a different drummer.

For a classic example of what Eeyore Politicizing

can do to a language, here's a not-so-brief-anymore passage from the "improved" Oregon Revised Statutes — one of many such passages rewritten to avoid "masculine" terms and voted into law:

> (a) When owned or leased by a farmer and used in transporting the farmer's own agricultural commodities, agricultural products or livestock . . . that were originally grown or raised by the farmer on the farm of the farmer, or when used in any transportation which is incidental to the regular operation of the farm of the farmer, or when used to transport supplies, equipment or materials to the farm of the farmer that are consumed or used on the farm of the farmer.

When all the books and so on have been censored and rewritten to suit the Eeyore Amazons, precisely what will have been accomplished? And why are *words* so important to them, anyway? For example, if they marry, they reject their husbands' family names. These names are paternal and are therefore symbols of "male chauvinism," they say. So they keep their unmarried names — which came from their fathers. (And their fathers were strong advocates of women's rights?)

Behind their antimasculine words, it's Overmasculinity as Usual, as the Eeyore Amazons imitate the lowest sort of masculine behavior and further the very energy they criticize. They break up Men's Clubs, which, they say, mean discrimination. Then they establish Women's Clubs, in which no men are allowed. They accuse men of being Sexists. Then they behave like Sexists. They say they want Sensitive Men. When they encounter such men, they shove them about. To put it plainly, *their* New Woman wants to be like the Old Man. And maybe even worse.

In a world that's practically screaming for relief from the Heavy Hand of Hypermasculinity, the Eeyore Amazons give us More of the Same. Who needs it? Countering Hypermasculinity with Hyper-masculinity is rather like dousing a fire by pouring gasoline on it. You can't *beat* sensitivity into people. But you can beat it out of them.

Into what sort of future, and what sort of world, are the Eeyore Amazons pushing us? Where is respect for the feminine going? As anyone can see, women are being Used and Abused more than ever. Never have they been portrayed so demeaningly in movies, television shows, magazines, and books. And, according to statistics, the feminine side of the work force is not being paid as much for its efforts as it was twenty years ago. The influence of the Eeyore Amazons may not exactly be setting femininity Free, but it *is* making it Remarkably Cheap.

If truth be told, respect for the feminine is sinking

like the *Titanic* – and, consequently, so is the state of the earth, the family, and society. The Eeyore Amazons blame men for all this. They might be wiser to blame misguided, excessive masculine energy – including that which they are advancing.

When the original *Titanic* went down, it was Women and Children First into the lifeboats. Now it's Women and Children Last. As a young man explained to us after a particularly nasty remark to his secretary, "We don't have to be nice to them anymore."

As do Eeyores in general, the Eeyore Amazons want men to stop being Chivalrous (not that many are now, anyway). Chivalry is Patronizing and De- meaning to Women, they say. But is it? And is chivalry limited to the behavior of men toward women? Whether of the European or the Asian variety, the code of chivalry makes kindness, consideration, and respect fashionable, and makes it admirable and desirable for the advantaged to assist the disadvantaged. Without chivalry, it's Claw and Fang, Might Makes Right, Kill or Be Killed. So we, along with past Taoist writers, knights-errant, and forest outlaws, would say: If you do away with chivalry, and do away with the feminine, Watch Out.

To close this chapter, we would like to quote from *Hope Against Hope: A Memoir*, in which Nadezhda

Mandelstam described the Eeyore Effect at work in Stalinist Russia. Unfortunately, the principle involved is not limited to another society at another time, but is universal and ever-present:

> There were once many kind people, and even unkind ones pretended to be good because that was the thing to do. Such pretense was the source of the hypocrisy and dishonesty so much exposed in the realist literature at the end of the last century. The unexpected result of this kind of critical writing was that kind people disappeared. Kindness is not, after all, an inborn quality – it has to be cultivated, and this only happens when it is in demand. For our generation, kindness was an old-fashioned, vanished quality, and its exponents were as extinct as the mammoth. Everything we have seen in our times – the . . . class warfare, the constant "unmasking" of people, the search for an ulterior motive behind every action – all this has taught us to be anything you like except kind.

How can one begin to overcome the Eeyore Within, and thereby begin to counteract the Eeyore Effect? We will get to that in a moment. But first . . .

The Tigger Tendency

It seems appropriate to begin this chapter with the Chinese story of "The Foolhardy Tiger":

> A large tiger was swaggering through the forest. Above his head, a small bird danced from branch to branch, singing. The tiger stopped and watched him. Then he called out:
>
> "What do you have to dance and sing about, you puny being? I am a thousand times larger than you. I can crush you in one paw, without even trying!"
>
> "Can you do this?" replied the bird, hopping lightly from one branch to another.
>
> "Of course I can!" roared the tiger. "Anything *you* can do, I can do better!" He leaped onto

the trunk, climbed high into the tree, then jumped out onto a branch. With a loud *crack*, it broke beneath his weight. So did the branches below it, all the way down. Ever so slowly, the bruised, rumpled tiger rose to his feet and staggered away.

Limping out of the woods, the tiger came to the edge of a field. There he saw a small, furry animal with weak eyes and funny-looking feet. At least, that's how they seemed to the tiger, who roared with laughter, forgetting his pain.

"What are you laughing at?" asked the mole, looking up at him.

"What odd little feet!" laughed the tiger. "And such weak little eyes!"

"I can see what I need to see," replied the mole, "and I can go where I need to go."

"Ho, ho, ho!" laughed the tiger. "I can do both of those things much better than you!"

"All right," said the mole. "Let's see you get past all those workers out there in the field." He disappeared down a hole, and shortly popped up from another hole beyond the farthest field hand.

"Here I come!" whooped the tiger, as he bounded into the field.

How the workers shouted! What heavy tools they

swung! What large rocks they threw! The scarred, battered tiger stumbled back the way he had come, barely escaping with his life.

After a while, he came to a swamp. And there he noticed a tiny, slow-moving creature with a curly shell on his back. "What a useless little thing!" exclaimed the tiger. "No legs at all!"

"What do I need legs for?" asked the snail. "There are many places legs cannot go."

"*Where?*" asked the incredulous tiger.

"Across this swamp, for example," replied the snail.

"Nonsense!" thundered the tiger. "I can cross it in an instant, by jumping from log to log!" And without a moment's hesitation, he leaped for the nearest log. Unfortunately, he was too heavy for that sort of thing, and fell short.

The snail slid slowly across on the grasses of the swamp, leaving the struggling tiger far behind.

"Talking is one thing," he remarked to himself. "*Doing* is another."

In this chapter, we look at Eeyore's Opposite – an animal who believes in *everything* and believes that everything is Something He Can Do. All things are possible to a Tigger, at least until he tries them.

"How did you get there, Roo?" asked Piglet.

"On Tigger's back! And Tiggers can't climb
downwards, because their tails get in the way,
only upwards, and Tigger forgot about that when
we started, and he's only just remembered. So
we've got to stay here for ever and ever – unless
we go higher. What did you say, Tigger? Oh,
Tigger says if we go higher we shan't be able to
see Piglet's house so well, so we're going to stop
here."

As anyone who's been around one knows, Tiggers
are first-rate at starting things, but are not very good
at completing them. Life is always greener elsewhere

to a Tigger once he's started something, and the Endless Possibilities constantly beckon – especially when he gets himself into a difficult situation, which is one thing Tiggers do quite easily.

> . . . Tigger was holding on to the branch and saying to himself: "[Jumping down]'s all very well for Jumping Animals like Kangas, but it's quite different for Swimming Animals like Tiggers." And he thought of himself floating on his back down a river, or striking out from one island to another, and he felt that that was really the life for a Tigger.
>
> "Come along," called Christopher Robin. "You'll be all right."
>
> "Just wait a moment," said Tigger nervously. . .
>
> "Come on, it's easy!" squeaked Roo. And suddenly Tigger found how easy it was.
>
> "Ow!" he shouted as the tree flew past him.

There's nothing wrong with being an Enthusiast. If it were not for enthusiasts, there would be no Major Advances in life, and very little excitement. But enthusiasts are more than Tiggers. They soon become well enough acquainted with whatever they're enthusiastic about to know when not to put their foot in it. Tigger is an *over*enthusiast. (And what *he* accomplishes is anybody's guess.)

In *The House at Pooh Corner*, Piglet described Tigger as "a Very Bouncy Animal, with a way of saying How-do-you-do, which always left your ears full of sand, even after Kanga had said, "Gently, Tigger dear," and had helped you up again." Rabbit described him as "the sort of Tigger who was always in front when you were showing him the way anywhere, and was generally out of sight when at last you came to the place and said proudly 'Here we are!' " Alexander Pope described him quite nicely when he wrote: "Some people never learn anything because they understand everything too quickly." A psychiatrist might describe him as "an impulse-driven personality." We would describe him as an animal with a whim of iron and the inner discipline of mush.

While the Teachings of the West tend to encourage Tigger's sort of behavior, the Teachings of the East contain many cautions against it. In the *Tao Te Ching*, for example, we find:

High winds do not blow all morning;
Heavy rain does not fall all day.
Are not these made by heaven and earth?
If the power of heaven and earth
Cannot make violent activity last,
How can you?

★ ★ ★

Standing on tiptoe, one is unsteady.
Taking long steps, one quickly tires.
Showing off, one shows unenlightenment.
Displaying self-righteousness, one reveals vanity.
Praising the self, one earns no respect.
Exaggerating achievements, one cannot long
    endure.
Followers of the Way consider these
Extra food, unnecessary baggage.
They bring no happiness.

Therefore, followers of the Way
Avoid them.

* ★ ★ ★ *

Do not conquer the world with force,
For force only causes resistance.
Thorns spring up when an army passes.
Years of misery follow a great victory.
Do only what needs to be done,
Without using violence.

* ★ ★ ★ *

It is not wise to dash about.
Shortening the breath causes stress.
Use too much energy, and
You will soon be exhausted.
That is not the Natural Way.
Whatever works against Tao
Will not last long.

"Going out, are you, Tigger?"

"Yes," he replied. "Roo and I are going on a picnic. I'm bringing the sandwiches."

"Oh? What's in that one?"

"Peanut butter, onions, mustard, and cheese."

"Oh. I . . . Er . . ."

"Is anything the matter?" asked Tigger. "You've gone green."

"No, it's nothing . . . Nothing at all. I'll be all right. I hope you're not going far."

"Why?" asked Tigger.

"Oh, just in case we have to bring Roo back suddenly."

"What for?"

"Nothing, nothing. Run along and enjoy yourselves. While you can."

Well, it takes all kinds to make a mess.

The West is full of Tiggers – restless seekers of instant gratification, larger-than-life overachievers. The West idolizes them because they're Bouncy and Exciting. Maybe even a bit *too* exciting. And they're becoming more exciting all the time. It seems that it's no longer adequate to be a True Individual, or even a Hero; now one needs to be some sort of Superman, living an overinflated life punctuated (in true Tigger fashion) with exclamation marks. *Faster than a speeding bullet! More powerful than a locomotive! Able to leap tall buildings in a single bound!* This is the age of Supereverything – Superstar, Superathlete, Supercoach, Superpolitician, even Superbusiness-man: *Faster than a speeding ticket! More powerful than a profit motive! Able to lease tall buildings in a single day!*

Tiggers are not necessarily what they seem, however. While they may appear to be self-propelled, they are in reality jerked this way and that by whatever immediately appealing object or sensation catches their attention. And while Tiggers may appear energetic to the extreme, their love of ceaseless action and sensation is actually a form of spiritual laziness. Tiggers are not in control of their lives, as is clearly shown by their behavior.

Unfortunately, it is quite easy to be an impatient, inconsiderate, scatterbrained Tigger in a society that admires, encourages, and rewards impulsive behavior. Advertisements tell us to buy whatever-it-is and Spoil ourselves. An appropriate word, *spoil*. We deserve it, they say. (Maybe we do, but we'd like to think we're better than that.) Store layouts are carefully designed to encourage impulse buying. Movies, television shows, and magazines promote impulsive behavior of the most questionable kind, in the most flash-it-in-their-faces manner. Practically everything from hair-styles to life-styles is endorsed as some sort of drug to be taken Now for Instant Relief. If you have this model of automobile, this style of clothing, this shape of girlfriend, or this sort of romantic entanglement, you will be happy. You will be loved. You will be Somebody. Those who can't have such things are doomed to frustration. Those who *can* have them are doomed to the inevitable disappointment. As Oscar Wilde put it, "In the world there are only two tragedies. One is not getting what one wants and the other is getting it." We are reminded of the old Persian curse: "May your every desire be immediately fulfilled."

In chapter twelve of the *Tao Te Ching*, Lao-tse described what's wrong with Tigger's sensation-alistic approach to life:

> *The five colors blind the eye.*
> *The five tones deafen the ear.*
> *The five flavors deaden the tongue.*
> *Racing and hunting madden the mind.*

While America is in many ways becoming Eeyore Country, in other ways it is turning into Tiggerland. A truly schizophrenic situation, one might say. The minds of American children are now so stressed and crippled by Tiggerish whambam Video Games, Television Shows, and Instant Left-Brain Computer Activities that many of them are unable to concentrate on anything for more than five minutes. As an ever-growing number of teachers are finding out, educating such minds is impossible. If something can't be immediately grasped, they won't understand it. And if it *can* be immediately grasped, they won't understand it, either — because Instant Information Accumulation is not *understanding*.

Perhaps today's children will be able to find employment years from now, anyway — they may be hired as technical laborers by the Chinese, Japanese, and Koreans, who will by then own just about everything because their cultures far more than ours encourage children to Focus the Mind.

The major lesson Tiggers need to learn is that if they don't control their impulses, their impulses will control them. No matter how much they do, Tiggers are never satisfied because they don't know the feeling of accomplishment that eventually comes when one persistently applies one's will to the attaining of not-immediately-reachable goals. The principle of this sort of achievement can be illustrated by the following story by Chuang-tse:

> K'ung Fu-tse and his followers were on their way to the state of Ch'u. As they emerged from a forest, they came upon a hunchback catching cicadas on the end of a stick as they flew by. "How skillful!" exclaimed the Master, stopping to watch. "Sir, what is your method?"
>
> "At first," the man answered, "I practiced balancing pellets on this stick. After five or six months, I

could handle two until they never fell down. Then I failed with only a few of the insects. I went on to three pellets. After that, I missed only one cicada in ten. By the time I could manipulate five pellets, I was catching cicadas without effort.

"When I focus my attention, my body becomes no more than a stump, and my arm the branch of a tree. Heaven and earth are great, and the ten thousand things multiply around me – but I pay no attention to them, only to the wings of the cicadas. My mind does not waver; my body maintains its balance. With such an attitude, how can I fail?"

K'ung Fu-tse turned and said to his disciples, "Remember the saying of old: 'When one's will is not distracted, one's power is increased.' How well has this gentleman demonstrated the truth of that today!"

Something else that Tiggers need to learn is found in the Japanese story of "The Samurai and the Zen Master":

A certain samurai had a reputation for impatient and hot-tempered behavior. A Zen master, well known for his excellent cooking, decided that the warrior needed to be taught a lesson before he became any more dangerous. He invited the samurai to dinner.

The samurai arrived at the appointed time. The Zen master told him to make himself comfortable while he finished preparing the food. A long time passed. The samurai waited impatiently. After a while, he called out: "Zen Master – have you forgotten me?"

The Zen master came out of the kitchen. "I am very sorry," he said. "Dinner is taking longer to prepare than I had thought." He went back to the kitchen.

A long time passed. The samurai sat, growing hungrier by the minute. At last he called out, a little softer this time: "Zen Master – please. When will dinner be served?"

The Zen master came out of the kitchen. "I'm sorry. There has been a further delay. It won't be much longer." He went back to the kitchen.

A long time passed. Finally, the samurai couldn't endure the waiting any longer. He rose to his feet, chagrined and ravenously hungry. Just then, the Zen master entered the room with a tray of food. First he served *miso shiru* (soybean soup).

The samurai gratefully drank the soup, enchanted by its flavor. "Oh, Zen Master," he exclaimed, "this is the finest *miso shiru* I have ever tasted! You truly deserve your reputation as an expert cook!"

"It's nothing," replied the Zen master, modestly. "Only *miso shiru.*"

The samurai set down his empty bowl. "Truly magical soup! What secret spices did you use to bring out the flavor?"

"Nothing special," the Zen master replied.

"No, no – I insist. The soup is extraordinarily delicious!"

"Well, there is one thing . . ."

"I knew it!" exclaimed the samurai, eagerly leaning forward. "There had to be *something* to make it taste so good! Tell me – what is it?"

The Zen master softly spoke: "It took *time*," he said.

"Tell me, Kanga – how has it been at your house since Tigger's been staying there?"

"Oh, it's been . . . *interesting.*"

"How do you mean?"

"Well, just yesterday morning, he knocked down the postman."

"Disgusting," said Owl, who had flown over to listen. "Absolutely disgusting."

"Why did he knock down the postman?"

"He thought he was taking something."

"Oh."

"Dis*gus*ting."

"You see, the postman carries a large sack – "

"Yes, yes. I hope Tigger apologized."

"He did. After I explained the situation."

"That's good."

"The postman was certainly decent about it."

"Oh? What did he say?"

"He said he'd been knocked down many a time by dogs – but never before by a *cat*."

The final problem we might mention about the Tigger Tendency is that the worthwhile and important things in life – wisdom and happiness in particular – are simply not the sorts of things one can Chase After and Grab. They are instead the sorts of things that come to us where we are, if we let them – if we stop trying too hard and just let things happen as they need to. Tigger found this out in spite of himself when he discovered What Tiggers Like Best, in the second chapter of *The House at Pooh Corner*.

Tigger had just come to the Forest and needed breakfast. So Pooh offered him some honey – being sure to ask, of course, if Tiggers *like* honey. "They like everything," Tigger cheerfully assured him. But it didn't take Tigger long to realize that . . .

"Tiggers don't like honey."

"Oh!" said Pooh, and tried to make it sound Sad and Regretful. "I thought they liked everything."

"Everything except honey," said Tigger.

Pooh felt rather pleased about this, and said that, as soon as he had finished his own breakfast, he would take Tigger round to Piglet's house, and Tigger could try some of Piglet's haycorns.

"Thank you, Pooh," said Tigger, "because haycorns is really what Tiggers like best."

So they went to see Piglet.

"Hallo, Piglet. This is Tigger."

"Oh, is it?" said Piglet, and he edged round to the other side of the table. "I thought Tiggers were smaller than that."

"Not the big ones," said Tigger.

"They like haycorns," said Pooh, "so that's what we've come for, because poor Tigger hasn't had any breakfast yet."

Piglet pushed the bowl of haycorns towards Tigger, and said: "Help yourself," and then he got close up to Pooh and felt much braver, and said, "So you're Tigger? Well, well!" in a careless sort of voice. But Tigger said nothing because his mouth was full of haycorns . . .

After a long munching noise he said:

"Ee-ers o i a-ors."

And when Pooh and Piglet said "What?" he said "Skoos ee," and went outside for a moment.

When he came back he said firmly:

"Tiggers don't like haycorns."

"But you said they liked everything except honey," said Pooh.

"Everything except honey and haycorns," explained Tigger.

When he heard this, Pooh said, "Oh, I see!" and Piglet, who was rather glad that Tiggers didn't like haycorns, said, "What about thistles?"

"Thistles," said Tigger, "is what Tiggers like best."

So they went to see Eeyore.

"Hallo, Eeyore!" said Pooh. "This is Tigger."

"What is?" said Eeyore.

"This," explained Pooh and Piglet together, and Tigger smiled his happiest smile and said nothing.

Eeyore walked all round Tigger one way, and then turned and walked all round him the other way.

"What did you say it was?" he asked.

"Tigger."

"Ah!" said Eeyore.

"He's just come," explained Piglet.

"Ah!" said Eeyore again.

He thought for a long time and then said:

"When is he going?"

Almost immediately, as it turned out.

"What's the matter?" asked Pooh.

"*Hot!*" mumbled Tigger . . .

"But you said," began Pooh — "you *said* that Tiggers liked everything except honey and haycorns."

"*And* thistles," said Tigger, who was now running round in circles with his tongue hanging out.

So they went to see *Kanga*. And when they had explained the situation to her, she kindly told Tigger to look in her cupboard to see what he'd like.

But the more Tigger put his nose into this and his paw into that, the more things he found which Tiggers didn't like. And when he had found everything in the cupboard, and couldn't eat any of it, he said to Kanga, "What happens now?"

But Kanga and Christopher Robin and Piglet were all standing round Roo, watching him have his Extract of Malt. And Roo was saying, "Must I?" and Kanga was saying, "Now, Roo dear, you remember what you promised."

"What is it?" whispered Tigger to Piglet.

"His Strengthening Medicine," said Piglet. "He hates it."

So Tigger came closer, and he leant over the back of Roo's chair, and suddenly he put out his tongue, and took one large golollop, and, with a sudden jump of surprise, Kanga said, "Oh!" and then clutched at the spoon again just as it was disappearing, and pulled it safely back out of Tigger's mouth. But the Extract of Malt had gone.

"Tigger *dear!*" said Kanga.

"He's taken my medicine, he's taken my medicine, he's taken my medicine!" sang Roo happily, thinking it was a tremendous joke.

Then Tigger looked up at the ceiling, and closed his eyes, and his tongue went round and round his chops, in case he had left any outside, and a peaceful smile came over his face as he said, "So *that's* what Tiggers like!"

And so –

★★★*CRASH*!!!!★★★

"Tigger, help the man up. That's Piglet's bodyguard you just knocked over. I mean, his *former* bodyguard."

"He's gone to sleep," said Tigger.

"No, I think he's unconscious. That was a little rough, wasn't it?"

"I was in a hurry," explained Tigger. "He got in the way."

"He must have come back for something. That's strange. I thought he'd gotten just about everything he could. Well, he won't get away this time."

"You're sorry about hitting his head with the floor, aren't you, Tigger? That's good."

Excuse me while I call the police.

Things As They
Might Be

By and by Piglet woke up. As soon as he woke he said to himself, "Oh!" Then he said bravely, "Yes," and then, still more bravely, "Quite so." But he didn't feel very brave, for the word which was really jiggeting about in his brain was "Heffalumps."

What was a Heffalump like?

Was it Fierce?

Did it come when you whistled? And *how* did it come?

Was it Fond of Pigs at all?

If it was Fond of Pigs, did it make any difference *what sort of Pig?*

Supposing it was Fierce with Pigs, would it make
any difference *if the Pig had a grandfather called
TRESPASSERS WILLIAM?*

In this chapter, we come from the illusions of
Eeyore and Tigger to those of Piglet, and to illusions
in general. To the Taoist, unhappiness is the result of
being guided by illusions – such as the mistaken belief
that man is something separate from the natural world.
Problems, be they economical, ecological, or whatever,
are caused by a failure to see What's There. Unpleasant
feelings come from illusions: fear from What Might
Be (which hasn't happened yet), sadness from What
Might Have Been (which is not necessarily what *would*
have been), and so on. Piglets, living in fear of What's
Coming Next, What Can Go Wrong, What If I Do
Something Foolish, and such, cannot enjoy and make
the most of the present moment. Later, they look
back and realize that they didn't *live* it. And that
realization makes them feel more inadequate than they
already did. However, because of their sensitivities,
their strong experience-filing-and-recalling memories,
and their cautious, one-step-at-a-time natures, Piglets
– far more than Eeyores and Tiggers, Rabbits and
Owls – have the ability to rise to a challenge and
accomplish the most difficult tasks, once interfering
illusions have been cleared away.

We will begin our examination of illusions with three narratives concerning the Perception of Situations, which show that It All Depends on How One Looks at Things. The first is by the Taoist writer Lieh-tse:

> A man noticed that his axe was missing. Then he saw the neighbor's son pass by. The boy looked like a thief, walked like a thief, behaved like a thief. Later that day, the man found his axe where he had left it the day before. The next time he saw the neighbor's son, the boy looked, walked, and behaved like an honest, ordinary boy.

The second example is the Chinese story of "The Well by the Road":

> A man dug a well by the side of a road. For years afterward, grateful travelers talked of the Wonderful Well. But one night, a man fell into it and drowned. After that, people avoided the Dreadful Well. Later it was discovered that the victim was a drunken thief who had left the road to avoid being captured by the night patrol — only to fall into the Justice-Dispensing Well.

> Same well; different views.

The third selection is from the writings of Chuang-tse:

> An archer competing for a clay vessel shoots effortlessly, his skill and concentration unimpeded. If the prize is changed to a brass ornament, his hands begin to shake. If it is changed to gold, he squints as if he were going blind. His abilities do not deteriorate, but his belief in them does, as he allows the supposed value of an external reward to cloud his vision.

Unfortunately, even the wise can occasionally go wrong by misinterpreting what's in front of them. In the third chapter of *Winnie-the-Pooh*, for example, a certain Wise but Overstuffed Bear —

"*Who's* Overstuffed?" said Pooh.

"All right, Pooh, you're not Overstuffed. You're Physically Superfluous."

"Oh, I wouldn't go *that* far," said Pooh modestly.

Anyway, Winnie-the-Pooh, whom most everyone calls Pooh, for short, was —

"No one calls me Pooh for Short," said Pooh. "Just Pooh."

Yes. All right . . . Winnie-the-Pooh, whom most everyone calls Just Pooh, was walking around and around in the snow near Piglet's house. When Piglet asked him what he was doing, he said he was Tracking something. He didn't know what. Possibly — just *possibly*, you know — it was a Woozle. Possibly it was more than that.

> "It's a very funny thing," said Bear, "but there seem to be *two* animals now. This — whatever-it-was — has been joined by another — whatever-it-is — and the two of them are now proceeding in company. Would you mind coming with me, Piglet, in case they turn out to be Hostile Animals?"

And Piglet, who ought to have known better, didn't. We mean, he did. Join him, that is.

There was a small spinney of larch trees just here, and it seemed as if the two Woozles, if that is what they were, had been going round this spinney; so round this spinney went Pooh and Piglet after them; Piglet passing the time by telling Pooh what his Grandfather Trespassers W had done to Remove Stiffness after Tracking, and how his Grandfather Trespassers W had suffered in his later years from Shortness of Breath, and other matters of interest, and Pooh wondering what a Grandfather was like, and if perhaps this was Two Grandfathers they were after now, and, if so, whether he would be allowed to take one home and keep it, and what Christopher Robin would say. And still the tracks went on in front of them . . .

Suddenly Winnie-the-Pooh stopped, and pointed excitedly in front of him. "*Look!*"

"*What?*" said Piglet, with a jump. And then, to show that he hadn't been frightened, he jumped up and down once or twice in an exercising sort of way.

"The tracks!" said Pooh. "*A third animal has joined the other two!*"

So — things were beginning to look Slightly Dangerous for Pooh and Piglet. But at least the third animal wasn't a Woozle. As Pooh pointed out, its prints

were different from the first two sets. They were
smaller.

> So they went on, feeling just a little anxious
> now, in case the three animals in front of them
> were of Hostile Intent ... And then, all of a
> sudden, Winnie-the-Pooh stopped again, and
> licked the tip of his nose in a cooling manner,
> for he was feeling more hot and anxious than
> ever in his life before. *There were four animals in
> front of them!*

The suspense was becoming unbearable. No, that's
not the word we want. What we mean is ...

> "I think," said Piglet, when he had licked the tip
> of his nose, too, and found that it brought very
> little comfort, "I *think* that I have just remembered
> something. I have just remembered something
> that I forgot to do yesterday and shan't be able

to do tomorrow. So I suppose I really ought to go back and do it now."

"We'll do it this afternoon, and I'll come with you," said Pooh.

"It isn't the sort of thing you can do in the afternoon," said Piglet quickly. "It's a very particular morning thing, that has to be done in the morning, and, if possible, between the hours of — What would you say the time was?"

"About twelve," said Winnie-the-Pooh, looking at the sun.

"Between, as I was saying, the hours of twelve and twelve five. So, really, dear old Pooh, if you'll excuse me — *What's that?*"

It was Christopher Robin, whistling to them from the branches of a nearby tree. What a relief.

"Silly old Bear," he said, "what *were* you doing? First you went round the spinney twice by yourself, and then Piglet ran after you and you went round again together, and then you were just going round a fourth time — "

Oh. So that's what it was. How embarrassing. Speaking of snow, we might also mention the time that Pooh and Piglet were out on a walk and decided to build a house for Eeyore in a sheltered spot in the pine wood by Eeyore's Gloomy Place. Of course, they needed something to build it with. Sticks would work nicely.

"There was a heap of sticks on the other side of the wood," said Piglet. "I saw them. Lots and lots. All piled up."

So they took the pile of sticks and made a house for Eeyore. And later, when Eeyore couldn't find his pile of – that is, when he couldn't find his house, he and Christopher Robin went looking for it, and met Pooh and Piglet, and . . .

"*Where* did you say it was?" asked Pooh.

"Just here," said Eeyore.

"Made of sticks?"

"Yes."

"Oh!" said Piglet.

"What?" said Eeyore.

"I just said 'Oh!' " said Piglet nervously. And so as to seem quite at ease he hummed Tiddely-pom once or twice in a what-shall-we-do-now kind of way.

"You're sure it *was* a house?" said Pooh. "I mean, you're sure the house was just here?"

"Of course I am," said Eeyore. And he murmured to himself, "No brain at all some of them."

"Why, what's the matter, Pooh?" asked Christopher Robin.

"Well," said Pooh . . . "The fact *is*," said Pooh . . . "Well, the fact *is*," said Pooh . . . "You see," said Pooh . . . "It's like this," said Pooh, and something seemed to tell him that he wasn't explaining very well, and he nudged Piglet again.

"It's like this," said Piglet quickly. . . . "Only warmer," he added after deep thought.

"What's warmer?"

"The other side of the wood, where Eeyore's house is."

So they went there, and Eeyore found his house, and . . .

So they left him in it; and Christopher Robin went back to lunch with his friends Pooh and Piglet, and on the way they told him of the Awful Mistake they had made. And when he had finished laughing, they all sang the Outdoor Song for Snowy Weather the rest of the way home . . .

How embarrassing.

"We're back," said Pooh.

"So you are. I was so busy writing that I didn't realize you'd gone."

"Piglet and I were just going over some Riddles," said Pooh. "Piglet has one for you."

"Very good, Piglet. What's your Riddle?"

"It's this," said Piglet. "What barks and has feathers?"

"Barks and has feathers? I . . . I don't know."

"A bird dog."

"Hmm."

"Is something wrong?" asked Piglet.

"All right, Piglet, here's one for you. What's the difference between a filing cabinet and a kangaroo?"

"I don't know," said Piglet.

"You don't? *You don't know the difference between a filing cabinet and a kangaroo?*"

"No," said Piglet.

"Well, then, I won't let you file any of *my* papers."

Silence.

"I don't get it," said Pooh.

In addition to the common human tendency to misinterpret What's There — as demonstrated by sometimes-a-little-too-human Pooh and Piglet in the snow just now — we might mention the inclination of a good many people to fail to notice anything but the unusual, as can be illustrated by the Chinese story of "The Ox and the Rat":

Many years ago Buddha called twelve animals before him, and told them that he would name a year of the Chinese zodiac after each. The animals were very pleased. But then the question of order arose, and trouble began.

"I should be first," said the rat, "because of my intelligence."

"No, *I* should be first," said the ox. "Because of my size."

The two animals argued for some time about which was more important, intelligence or size. After a while, the rat fell silent. "All right," he said at last, "I admit that size is more important." "Good," said the ox. "It's settled." "Not so fast," said the rat. "My size is more impressive than yours." "*What?*" snorted the indignant ox. "How can you, a mere rodent, impress anyone with your size?" "Let us go before the people," replied the rat, "and let the opinion of the majority decide." "Ridiculous!" the ox exclaimed. "Why should we waste time on your nonsense? Anyone can see that — "

"Now, now," said Buddha. "Let's not argue about it any longer. Of course the rat is smaller than you are. But why not let the majority of the people decide? Whoever more impresses them with his size shall be declared the winner." The ox, certain of victory, agreed.

"Lord Buddha," said the rat. "With the consent of the ox, I wish to have one favor granted before we present ourselves. If I am truly as small as the ox insists I am, I should like to lessen my inevitable embarrassment. Therefore, I ask that you temporarily double my size."

Buddha asked the ox if he had any objections. "Of course not," the ox answered. "After all, how much difference could it make? I'd still be one hundred times bigger than he is!"

The ox and the rat, the rat now twice his ordinary size, went out and walked among the crowds. Everywhere they went, people exclaimed in amazement. "Look at the size of that rat!" they shouted. "*Look at that enormous rat!*" No one noticed the ox. Everyone had seen an ox before. There was nothing unusual about him.

And that is how the rat impressed the people with his size, and became the first animal in the Chinese zodiac.

"By the way, Piglet, I've been thinking about that sign by your house . . ."

"You mean 'TRESPASSERS W'?"

"Yes. That was your grandfather's name, you said."

"Yes – Trespassers William."

"Well, he must have been a rather large pig, to put up such a tall sign."

"Er . . . Well . . . He didn't put it up himself. A friend did it for him."

"A friend?"

"Yes, another sort of animal. A *tall* sort of animal."

"You mean, like a giraffe?"

"Yes, yes — a giraffe. That was it."

"It must have been an amusing friendship, a pig and a giraffe. I didn't know giraffes could be found around here."

"They can't," said Piglet. "Ordinarily. But this giraffe was over here on an Exchange Program."

"Oh? What did we send in exchange?"

"Er . . . A box of weasels."

"That doesn't sound like a very fair exchange."

"Well, it was a *large* box."

Yes, well . . . Speaking of Illusions, let's return to that subject. We believe there are a few things more to be said.

Although Illusions exist all over the world, the Industrial West seems to have more than a fair share of them. And the Illusions of the West — which of course by now have been exported to the East — deserve to be watched out for with special care. It seems rather ironic, somehow, that "realistic," "scientific" Western industrial society sneers at the relatively harmless myths and acquired beliefs of the native peoples of the world – a good many of which have at least some basis in fact – while perpetuating irrational beliefs and practices so dangerous that they are destroying the earth. And probably the most destructive of all the Illusions of the West is the superstitious notion that Technology will solve all our difficulties.

This Technology Worship could be said to have started in Western Europe in the 1500s or so, with Explorations and Expansions that led to the growth of Commercialism, which led to the Industrial Revolution of the 1700s. The rapid proliferation of Hungry Machines, and the accompanying breakneck exploitation of natural resources with which to feed them, quickly transformed rural, agricultural societies – "Good morning, Mrs. Witherspoon! What a lovely cow!" – into city and factory societies ("I certainly hope – gasp, wheeze – we don't run out of – cough – *coal* before the day is over!") and then into big city, big industry societies: "That's right, Inspector – *they stole everything that wasn't fastened to the floor!*" In the Victorian era, this Industrial Fanaticism was given a large boost by empire-and-opinion makers who believed that science could do anything, and that any opinions to the contrary were heresy.

But well before then, some similar pillage-the-earth-and-let's-have-no-nonsense-about-it nonsense had been exported from Europe to the New World. And with it came the absurd and groundless belief that money could buy happiness. It would have been rather surprising if such a belief had *not* arrived on these shores, considering that a good many of the earliest immigrants were debtors from English prisons, fur trappers, tobacco and cotton barons-to-be, and Puritan tradesmen. Such people tended to know enough about the natural world to exploit it, but not much more — if indeed they knew even that. The Puritans in particular knew next to nothing about how to get along in the North American forests, meadows, and mountains, and next to nothing about how to get along with the people who did. As the old saying puts it, "They fell first upon their knees, and then upon the Indians." And then upon the landscape. As Luther Standing Bear, chief of the Oglala Sioux, described the situation:

> We did not think of the great open plains, the beautiful rolling hills, and winding streams with tangled growth, as "wild." Only to the white man was nature a "wilderness" and only to him was the land "infested" with "wild" animals and "savage" people. To us it was tame. Earth was bountiful and we were surrounded with the

blessings of the Great Mystery. Not until the hairy
man from the east came and with brutal frenzy
heaped injustices upon us and the families we
loved was it "wild" for us. When the very animals
of the forest began fleeing from his approach,
then it was that for us the "Wild West" began.

Today, thanks to this rather lopsided cultural
foundation, we live in what is commonly described
as a Materialistic Society. But that description is in
error. Ours is in reality an Abstract Value society –
one in which things are not appreciated for what they
are so much as for what they *represent*. If Western
industrial society appreciated the Material World, there
would be no junkyards, no clearcut forests, no shoddily
designed and manufactured products, no poisoned
water sources, no obese, fuel-guzzling automobiles,
nor any of the other horrors and eyesores that haunt
us at every turn. If ours were a materialistic society,
we would love the physical world – and we would
know our limits within it.

In truth, Western industrial society does not even
notice the Material World. It quickly discards it, leaves
it to rust in the rain. The material world is Here and
Now, and industrial society does not appreciate or
pay attention to the Here and Now. It's too busy
coveting and rushing after the There and Later On.

As a result, it all too often fails to see what is right in front of it, and what's coming from that. It forgets where it has been; it does not know where it is going.

> "Going on an Expotition?" said Pooh eagerly. "I don't think I've ever been on one of those. Where are we going to on this Expotition?"
>
> "Expedition, silly old Bear. It's got an 'x' in it."
>
> "Oh!" said Pooh. "I know." But he didn't really.
>
> "We're going to discover the North Pole."
>
> "Oh!" said Pooh again. "What *is* the North Pole?" he asked.
>
> "It's just a thing you discover," said Christopher Robin carelessly, not being quite sure himself.

Perhaps the preceding glimpse at our historical conditioning can help to explain why Western industrial society has such a poor record when it comes to observing What's There. In our part of the world, this unobservant tendency is displayed in the most depressing manner whenever there's an Election. For nearly thirty years now, the nation that was once the Light of the Free World has been electing to the highest office in the land a succession of Nightmare Clowns who lead us deeper and deeper into darkness as they encourage massive greed and corruption, run up multibillion-dollar debts for future generations to pay, turn the economy into jelly, refuse to take action necessary to save what's left of the natural world ("More studies are needed"), and threaten to blow up the planet because some country somewhere isn't doing what they think it ought to quickly enough – all the while making remarks on the intelligence level of "If you've seen one redwood tree, you've seen them all."

And speaking of trees, if the majority of voters are not living in some sort of fantasy, why this increasing tendency to talk about Protecting the Environment while voting more than ever against it? In a recent election in our once-almost-environmentalist home state, for example, the majority voted to allow one of the nation's most notoriously unsafe and unnecessary nuclear power plants to continue operation despite its persistent violation of vital safety regulations; rejected a measure that would have restricted throwaway packaging; and turned down an honest, self-funded, pro-environment political candidate to re-elect a politician who for years has actively opposed the preservation of what little remains of the state's uncut forests, who supports the timber industry's policy of clearcutting public lands and sending the logs overseas for processing (thereby shutting down local mills), and who has annually appended to appropriations bills riders forbidding citizens from challenging this policy in court. So much for Planet Earth.

The natural world is all right, voters across the country seem to be saying, as long as its preservation doesn't interfere with the process of destroying it to earn money. Let Someone Else pay for its protection. But, considering that less than 1 percent of American philanthropic giving goes to conservation, it would appear that Someone Else is just another fantasy.

> "We're all going on an Expotition with Christopher Robin!"
>
> "What is it when we're on it?"
>
> "A sort of boat, I think," said Pooh.
>
> "Oh! That sort."
>
> "Yes. And we're going to discover a Pole or something. Or was it a Mole? Anyhow we're going to discover it."

Unfortunately for our chances of survival and happiness, we in the West have inherited an Eeyore version of religion, which denounces the world as an evil place whose ways are to be ignored by the wise, and an Eeyore sort of science, which sneers at anything beyond a mechanistic view of the earth – the secrets of which it attempts to sneak out of it bit by bit, for the purpose of manipulating the natural world. Is either of these Ways very likely to get us out of the mess we're in? Or to even help us see what's causing it?

Eeyore religion says that the earth isn't worth saving, anyway, and that when it comes to an end, the Faithful will be transported instantly to heaven. No problem. We'd like to see them explain things to Saint Peter at the Gate, when he asks them what they did with the world that God entrusted to them. *That* might get a bit sticky.

Eeyore science, on the other hand, insists that Technology will rescue us from destruction – including the considerable destruction that Technology causes. When it tells us things like that, we can't help but wonder if it isn't trying to be some sort of religion itself. No, not a religion, exactly – some sort of *voodoo*.

"*Wunga wunga, moomba noonga* – Great Tin God, save us from hexachlorobenzene, ethylene dibromide, toxaphene, chlordane, parathion, and everything else you've given us that's gone wrong." Well, *wunga wunga*, everybody – and lots of luck!

"Oh! Piglet," said Pooh excitedly, "we're going

on an Expotition, all of us, with things to eat. To discover something."

"To discover what?" said Piglet anxiously.

"Oh! just something."

"Nothing fierce?"

"Christopher Robin didn't say anything about fierce. He just said it had an 'x'."

"It isn't their necks I mind," said Piglet earnestly. "It's their teeth . . ."

The fearful fantasies we have inherited have conditioned us to believe that we need to be protected from the natural world. Better Living Through Heavy Industry, and so on. In reality, as anyone ought to be able to see by now, the natural world needs to be protected from us. Its wisdom needs to be recognized, respected, and understood by us, and not merely viewed through the distorted lenses of our illusions about it. As Sir Arthur Conan Doyle cautioned, through his character Sherlock Holmes, "One's ideas must be as broad as Nature if they are to interpret Nature," and "When one tries to rise above Nature one is liable to fall below it." Chuang-tse's words to that effect have a timely ring:

When leaders pursue knowledge but do not follow the Way, all who follow them become lost in confusion. How can I say this is so?

Much knowledge is applied in the making of bows, crossbows, arrows, and slingshots, but the birds in the air are disturbed and injured by it. Much knowledge is used in making hooks, nets, and other such devices, but the fish in the waters are disturbed and injured by it. Much knowledge is utilized in the design and placement of traps, meshes, and snares, but the creatures of the ground are disturbed and injured by it.

As knowledge becomes increasingly clever, versatile, and artful, the people all around are disturbed and injured by it. They then struggle to grasp what they do not know, but make no attempt to grasp what they know already. They condemn the misunderstanding of others, but do not condemn their own. From this more confusion comes.

If the sun and moon lost their light, the mountains and rivers abandoned their vitality, and the four seasons came to an end, no insect or plant would retain its true nature. Yet this is the condition produced in men by an obsession for knowledge. Honesty and simplicity are overlooked, and restlessness is admired. Quiet, effortless action is forgotten, and loud quarreling is

heard. Such is the nature of hunger for knowledge. Its noise throws the world into chaos.

We might add some other words by Chuang-tse:

> Men honor what lies within the sphere of their
> knowledge, but do not realize how dependent
> they are on what lies beyond it.

To illustrate the vital truth of that last statement,
we have decided to give a very brief history of what
we call Popular Radiation.

In the 1930s, as people were dying from the effects
of radium-laced Health Tonics, the U.S. government
established its first maximum level of tolerable
exposure to radiation. Just in case, you know.

In the 1940s, following study of Hiroshima
bombing victims, that level was halved. Just to be safe,
you understand.

In the 1950s, in response to concern over nuclear-
bomb-testing fallout, which seemed to be affecting
some people in unpleasant ways, the maximum
tolerable level was substantially lowered. Just as a
precaution.

At the same time, however, utility company
advertisements were extolling the charms of the
newest form of power generation — "clean, safe"

nuclear energy. Their billboards invited customers to
"Take the Family to the Nuclear Power Park." X-ray
machines were being used in shoe stores to examine
children's feet. And people were having their sup-
posedly-enlarged-but-actually-normal thymus glands
irradiated. Like many exposed to radiation before
them, a sizable number of these people developed
cancer and died.

In the 1960s, more and more people came to
suspect that they weren't being told the Whole Truth
about this sort of thing. And then . . .

In the 1970s, researchers reported that Americans
were being exposed to nine times more radiation from
medical applications than from atmospheric nuclear
fallout – which by then, due in part to studies of
certain Nevada residents and military personnel, was
being connected with all sorts of problems. In 1979,
the Three Mile Island nuclear power facility broke
down and irradiated the surrounding area.

In the 1980s, new data on the Hiroshima victims
and their descendants showed that the risk of cancer
from radiation was up to fifteen times greater than
authorities had previously believed. Emissions from
nuclear plants were linked with thyroid damage,
miscarriages, and other health problems. And before
the end of the decade, the Chernobyl nuclear facility,
like Three Mile Island before it, had done what experts

in the field had said it wouldn't do in a thousand years. Reports of near-disasters at other plants were being leaked to the press . . . So the "safe exposure" level was lowered again. Not taking any chances.

At each step of the way, authorities assured the public that the New Devices and New Amounts of radiation were safe. And each time, they were wrong.

Today the public is being captivated by computers, word processors, and the like – whose cathode ray tubes emit X-ray radiation, and whose circuits and display terminals produce strong electromagnetic fields. They're perfectly safe, authorities assure us. And if any difficulties *should* happen to develop, we will certainly be notified later on.

The latest Popular Radiation devices is the Microwave Oven, which bombards food with high-frequency electromagnetic radiation, irritating it until it heats up. This sort of Perversion of Nature is perfectly safe, authorities insist – if it weren't, the Wonderful Machines wouldn't be on the market. Maybe the authorities are correct this time, just for once. On the other hand, maybe they're not.

> As soon as he had finished his lunch Christopher Robin whispered to Rabbit, and Rabbit said, "Yes, yes, of course," and they walked a little way up the stream together.

"I didn't want the others to hear," said Christopher Robin.

"Quite so," said Rabbit, looking important.

"It's — I wondered — It's only — Rabbit, I suppose *you* don't know, What does the North Pole *look* like."

"Well," said Rabbit, stroking his whiskers. "Now you're asking me."

"I did know once, only I've sort of forgotten," said Christopher Robin carelessly.

"It's a funny thing," said Rabbit, "but I've sort of forgotten too, although I did know *once*."

"I suppose it's just a pole stuck in the ground?"

"Sure to be a pole," said Rabbit, "because of calling it a pole, and if it's a pole, well, I should think it would be sticking in the ground, shouldn't you, because there'd be nowhere else to stick it."

"Yes, that's what I thought."

"The only thing," said Rabbit, "is *where is it sticking?*"

"That's what we're looking for," said Christopher Robin.

"Say, Piglet — what's that at the window?"

"*It's the Heffalump!*" cried Piglet, jumping straight up in alarm.

"Oh − it's the garbageman, taking away the recycling. You didn't really think it was a Heffalump, did you?"

"No (pant, pant). Not (pant) really."

"Now, Piglet. What if it *had* been a Heffalump? What could he have done to you?"

"I don't know," squeaked Piglet. "But he might have thought of *something*."

"You don't even know what a Heffalump is, do you?"

"No . . . Not exactly."

"You don't even know if Heffalumps *exist*."

"Well, do they?"

"Not in this part of the world, anyway − not lurking about outside the window."

"Are you sure?"

"Absolutely. You won't find a Heffalump around here any more than you'll find a giraffe putting up a sign by your house."

"Oh," said Piglet. "I see."

Where were we? Oh, yes − dangerous illusions. In his amazingly Taoist-like *Magical Child*, Joseph Chilton Pearce described our society's predicament this way:

How do we believe that we can predict and control the natural forces of the universe? Through clever intellectual manipulations and tool usage. We accept this notion so completely because we have been conditioned to believe implicitly that only by so using our intelligence can we, in fact, survive nature. Interaction between the mind-brain and its source of information [the earth] has been rigorously, religiously denied by Western logic, if not *most* cultural logic. Interaction with the living earth would imply that the earth responded in kind, interacting with us. And the one cardinal rule of all classical Western academic belief . . . is that the mind has absolutely no relation to the world other than to be informed of that world through the senses and to make some sort of intelligent reaction to that information. This belief has automatically robbed us of personal power. Having no personal power to draw on, we are reduced to only one source of power: tool usage. And so, we have evolved a continuing body of knowledge concerning the employment, creation, enhancement, and service of tools. Our real criterion of value becomes the culture's body of knowledge offering or promising enhanced tool production, possible domination of nature, and so some security. *Potential is seen as an increase of tools.* [our emphasis] The training and education of children is designed to lead to better tool invention, production, consumption, and handling.

Our body of knowledge and tool development has never given, is not presently giving, and almost surely will never give us either physical security or well-being. The more vast and awesome our tool production has become, the greater our anxiety, hostility, fear, resentment, and aggression. But the direct correlation between our anxiety and tool production is almost beyond our grasp because our intelligence is itself the result of our conditioning by and within that very body of knowledge. Our intelligence is trained to believe that any imperfections in the reality resulting from our activities, such as personal anguish, misery, and fear, simply indicate the need for improvements in the body of knowledge and/or improvements in tool production, distribution, and application. Even as our body of knowledge splits us off from our lives and creates anxiety and unhappiness, it conditions us to believe religiously that escape from our misery lies in perfecting that body of knowledge.

In other words, modern man's difficulties, dangerous beliefs, and feelings of loneliness, spiritual emptiness, and personal weakness are caused by his illusions about, and separation from the natural world.

Well, the Taoists told us this sort of mess would happen. And they told us what we could do about it. Now it's time to see what that is.

Things As They Are

On the 10th of September last, I walked down
the Via Salaria and into the Republic of Utopia,
a quiet country lying eighty years east of Fara
Sabina. Noticing the cheerful disposition of the
inhabitants, I enquired the cause of their contentment, and I was told that it was due to their laws
·and to the teaching they received from their
earliest school days. . . .

In order to teach small children to observe
particulars they practise a kind of game, in which
a number of small objects, e.g., three grains of
barley, a small coin, a blue button . . . are con-
cealed in the hand. The hand is opened for an
instant, then quickly closed again, and the child
is asked to say what it has seen. For older children
the game is gradually made more elaborate, until

finally they all know how their hats and shoes are made. I was also informed that by learning how to define words these people have succeeded in defining their economic terms, with the result that various iniquities of the stock market and financial world have entirely disappeared from their country, for no one allows himself to be fooled any longer.

These very Taoist words are from *Gold and Work*, by Ezra Pound. But the principle they describe – that of Reality Appreciation – is a great deal older. Before we present some *official* Taoist writings on that sort of thing, we would like to quote from our favorite *un*official Taoist writer, Henry David Thoreau:

Shams and delusions are esteemed for soundest truths, while reality is fabulous. If men would steadily observe realities only, and not allow themselves to be deluded, life, to compare it with such things as we know, would be like a fairy tale and the Arabian Nights' Entertainments. . . . By closing the eyes and slumbering, and consenting to be deceived by shows, men establish and confirm their daily life of routine and habit everywhere, which still is built on purely illusory foundations. Children, who play life, discern its true law and relations more clearly than men, who fail to live it worthily, but who think that they are wiser by experience, that is, by failure.

. . . Men esteem truth remote, in the outskirts of the system, behind the farthest star, before Adam and after the last man. In eternity there is indeed something true and sublime. But all these times and places and occasions are now and here. God himself culminates in the present moment, and will never be more divine in the lapse of all the ages. And we are enabled to apprehend at all what is sublime and noble only by the perpetual instilling and drenching of the reality that surrounds us.

Out of the "Hundred Schools" of Chinese philosophy, only two – Confucianism and Taoism – have survived. They have lasted through thousands of years because they have proven the most Useful. The Chinese are very practical people – they have no respect for things that sound good but don't work. In the East generally, and in China especially, philosophy has always been considered of no value unless it can be, and is, applied in one's daily life.

Western philosophy, having little connection with everyday living, is (to this observer, at least) comparatively egocentric and impractical, with much Arguing and Theorizing, and much bounding back and forth across the intellectual landscape – a pleasant, part-time diversion formulated by and aimed at the likes of Owl, Rabbit, and sometimes Eeyore, but not particularly supportive of the likes of Piglet and Pooh. Western philosophy has become the domain of pipe-smoking, tweed-suited college professors (who may profess it but not necessarily practice it) and hyper-cerebral students who, for all their intelligence, often seem to have a hard time washing their clothes or repairing the lawn mower.

Looking askance at all this, the typical Mind of the West says: So who needs *Eastern* philosophy? To such a mind, Eastern philosophy has two things wrong with it. First, it's Eastern – exotic and mystical, quaint but useless. Second, it's Philosophy. And what good does *that* do anybody?

What this narrow-minded attitude overlooks is the fact that much of what makes up the Practical West came from the East, and most of that came from China. And, we might add, a good deal of it came from the Taoists – China's foremost scientists, inventors, medical men, artists, and observers of the natural world.

In the West we are told in school that Johann Gutenberg invented movable type, William Harvey discovered the circulation of the blood, and Sir Isaac Newton was the originator of his First Law of Motion. In reality, these things were invented and discovered in China long before those men were born. In addition to who-knows-how-many other things, the

Chinese have given the world the mechanical clock, paper (including wall-paper, toilet paper, paper handkerchiefs, money, and playing cards), multicolor printing, porcelain, lacquer, phosphorescent paint, the magic lantern (ancestor of the movie projector), the spinning wheel, the wheelbarrow, the umbrella, the modern plow, harness, seed drill, and rotary winnowing fan (as well as the practice of growing crops in rows), the fishing reel, the modern compass (and the difference between true and magnetic north), the seismograph, relief and grid maps, the decimal system, the calculator, the hermetically sealed research laboratory, the chain drive, the belt drive, the chain pump, the essentials of the steam engine, dial and pointer devices, cast iron, the manufacture of steel from cast iron, the suspension bridge, the segmental arch (non-semi-circle) bridge, the contour transport canal, the canal pound-lock, masts, sails, the rudder, watertight compartments in ships, the paddle-wheel boat, land sailing, the kite (including the acrobatic kite, the fighter kite, the message kite, the musical kite, the lighted kite . . .), the hang glider (which, like the acrobatic kite, was developed and flown by Taoist adepts in the mountains of China as a way to learn and work with natural laws), the hot-air balloon, the helicopter rotor, the parachute (fifteen hundred years before Leonardo da Vinci's), tuned bells, "church" (court and temple) bells, equal temperament in music (championed one hundred and thirty-eight years later in the West by Johann Sebastian Bach), drilling for natural gas, the butane gas cylinder (in its original form, a gas-filled bamboo tube with a valve at one end, over which travelers cooked their food on journeys), sunglasses, waterproof clothing, mountain-climbing gear, and gunpowder (which, ironically, was discovered by a Taoist searching for the formula to an elixir of longevity). A group of court ladies invented matches, which were brought to Europe one thousand years later. Some other Chinese discovered the structure of snowflakes – two thousand years ahead of the West – and the existence of sunspots and solar wind. The Chinese discovered diabetes and deficiency diseases and pioneered the sciences of endocrinology, immunology, thyroid hormone therapy, and anatomy (deducing, among other things, the presence and design of the eardrum before its physical discovery). They developed systems of biological pest control . . . Well, that ought to be enough to make the point. These people Noticed things.

Unfortunately, one thing the West did *not* import from the East was the traditional Chinese belief that science, morality, and spirituality must go together; that science without ethical and spiritual considerations was not a whole science, but a form of madness. Oh, well – we can't have everything, we suppose.

Returning to Pooh and friends, this business of scientific observation and so on reminds us of the quite Taoist discovery of the principle of Poohsticks, a game that has been played around the world ever since it was described in *The House at Pooh Corner* (and just *possibly* before). Pooh, as you may remember, had been studying fir-cones and had made up a rhyme about one in particular . . .

He had just come to the bridge; and not looking where he was going, he tripped over something, and the fir-cone jerked out of his paw into the river.

"Bother," said Pooh, as it floated slowly under the bridge, and he went back to get another fir-cone which had a rhyme to it. But then he thought that he would just look at the river instead, because it was a peaceful sort of day, so he lay down and looked at it, and it slipped slowly away beneath him . . . and suddenly, there was his fir-cone slipping away too.

"That's funny," said Pooh. "I dropped it on the other side," said Pooh, "and it came out on this side! I wonder if it would do it again?" And he went back for some more fir-cones.

It did. It kept on doing it. Then he dropped two in at once, and leant over the bridge to see which of them would come out first; and one of them did; but as they were both the same size, he didn't know if it was the one which he wanted to win, or the other one. So the next time he dropped one big one and one little one, and the big one came out first, which was what he had said it would do, and the little one came out last, which was what he had said it would do, so he had won twice . . . and when he went home for tea, he had won thirty-six and lost twenty-eight, which meant that he was – that he had – well, you take twenty-eight from thirty-six, and *that's* what he was. Instead of the other way around.

And that was the beginning of the game called Poohsticks, which Pooh invented, and which he and his friends used to play on the edge of the Forest. But they played with sticks instead of fircones, because they were easier to mark.

In that Poohishly humble incident, one can see all the elements of pure science as practiced by the Taoists: the chance occurrence, the observant and inquisitive mind, deduction of the principles involved, application of those principles, modification of materials, and a new practice or way of doing things. Not bad. But after all, Pooh is *That* sort of Bear.

As we have already implied, there is a good deal more to the Importance of Observation than scientific discoveries. There is also the matter of Living Wisely and Well. In this area in particular, we believe, the West could learn a few things from the East. For example, what sort of education in Practical Wisdom do we tend to receive in school?

> There are three hundred cows in a field. The gate has been left open, and two cows pass through it every minute. How many cows are left in the field after an hour and a half?

This sort of thing, we're told, will help us once we graduate – help us apply our learning to everyday matters and, ideally, help us discern the true from the false. But, to return to the terms of the three-hundred-cow math problem: If you have ever herded cattle, you know that cows do not pass through an open gate at the rate of two per minute. They either go through all at once, or not at all. Or they wander through whenever they feel up to it. In all probability, there would be *no* cows left in the field *ten minutes* after a gate was opened, or a fence pulled down. But if you told the teacher that, you would be told that you were wrong. Such is the difference between School and Life. (And if you in school don't believe that such a difference exists, just wait until you get out.)

If we were asked to condense Taoist teachings regarding everyday life to their irreducible essentials, we would say: Observe, Deduce, and Apply. Watch what is around you — putting aside, as best you can, previous conceptions that you or others might have about it. Ideally, look at it as though you were seeing it for the first time. Mentally reduce it to its basic elements — "See simplicity in complexity," as Lao-tse put it. Use intuition as well as logic in order to understand what you see (a vital difference between the Whole Reasoner and the Left-Brain Technician). Look for connections between one thing and another — notice patterns and relationships. Study the natural laws you see operating through them. Then work with those laws, applying the smallest possible amount of interference and effort, in order to learn more and achieve whatever you need to — and no more.

Once you make a habit of Observing, Deducing,

and Applying, you may sense a pathway opening up ahead of you – or inside of you, or both – leading to a deeper understanding of things. You may even feel at times as though you're in some sort of Other Dimension, like Thoreau's example of the Arabian Nights' Entertainments. But you're not, really; you're just seeing and experiencing Things As They Are, rather than as someone-or-other *says* they are. And the difference between the two can be considerable.

In a sense, though, the image of another dimension is an appropriate one. For as you follow the Way, you leave the land of Either/Or and enter the land of Both. As Lao-tse wrote in the first chapter of the *Tao Te Ching*, many people are unable to follow the Way because they are unable to *see* it, being stuck in Either/Or:

> *Those habitually without desires*
> *Perceive [the Way] as "subtlety."*
> *Those habitually with desires*
> *Perceive it as "action."*
> *These two have the same source,*
> *But different names.*
> *Together they're called "darkness"–*
> *Darkness of increasing darkness,*
> *All mystery's gateway.*

In other words, Tao is both "subtlety" and "action." Those who consider it only as spirit and ignore its forms, or who notice its forms but disregard what is behind and within them, know of only half of it, at best — neither the Spiritual people who deny the world nor the Physical people who deny the spirit can know of and follow the Way. But *you* can.

"I feel dizzy," said Piglet, who had been reading over my shoulder.

"Yes, I did get a bit carried away, didn't I?"

"Isn't there some other way of explaining all that?"

"I suppose. Let's try it like this . . ."

Taoism is not the reject-the-physical-world way of living that some scholars (and a few Taoists) would have others believe. Even Lao-tse, the most reclusive of Taoist writers, wrote, "Honor all under heaven as your body." To a Taoist, a reject-the-physical-world approach would be an extremist absurdity, impossible to live — without dying. Instead, a Taoist might say: Carefully observe the natural laws in operation in the world around you, and live by them. From following them, you will learn the morality of modesty, moderation, compassion, and consideration (not just one society's rules and regulations), the wisdom of seeing things as they are (not of merely collecting "facts" about them), and the happiness of being in harmony with the Way (which has nothing to do with self-righteous "spiritual" obsessions and fanaticism). And you will live lightly, spontaneously, and effortlessly.

"Well, Piglet?"

"Could you tell some stories?"

"Yes, I suppose I could."

"Stories?" said Pooh, opening his eyes.

"I *would* like to hear some stories," said Piglet.

"So would I," said Pooh. "All seriousness aside."

"All . . . Yes. All seriousness aside. Let's see — we were just mentioning observation, spontaneity, and effortlessness . . . Would you like to hear 'The Old Master and the Horse'?"

"We won't know," said Pooh, "until we've heard it."

"True enough. This is how it goes . . ."

A horse was tied outside a shop in a narrow Chinese village street. Whenever anyone would try to walk by, the horse would kick him. Before long, a small crowd of villagers had gathered near the shop, arguing about how best to get past the dangerous horse. Suddenly, someone came running. "The Old Master is coming!" he shouted. "*He'll* know what to do!"

> The crowd watched eagerly as the Old Master
> came around the corner, saw the horse, turned,
> and walked down another street.

"You see," I said, "the Old Master lived the principle of *Wu Wei*, or Effortless Action. That's something the Taoists say we can learn by watching water."

"Water?" asked Piglet.

"When a stream comes to some stones in its path, it doesn't struggle to remove them, or fight against them, or *think* about them. It just goes around them. And as it does, it sings. Water responds to What's There with effortless action."

"I think I missed something," said Pooh.

"Missed something where?" I asked.

"In the story —"

"Oh, that. The Old Master knew he didn't have to go down that street. He knew he could go another way."

"But why didn't the others know?"

"Ah! Precisely. Why *didn't* they know?"

"*I* wouldn't have gone down that street," squeaked Piglet. "Not with a horse in the way. Or a goat. Or a dog. Or anything."

"But why didn't the others — "

"My dear Pooh," said Owl, flying over to the

writing table. "In problems of this sort, one must consider the Physical Properties involved."

"I didn't know there were any," replied Pooh, rubbing his ear.

"*That is to say*," continued Owl, somewhat annoyed, "the street in question was narrow, the horse was large – and furthermore it was Belligerent."

"Further along it was what?"

"It kicked. The Old Master knew that it was Futile to Proceed – "

"We know that, Owl," I said. "The point is – "

Oh, well – so much for stories. Let's go on to the next principle.

When you observe the natural world, you'll eventually see that everything in it is designed to succeed – including what some might judge to be "bad." If you want to learn the natural world's principles of success, you'll need to see things not as "good" or "bad," but as they are. This does not mean discard morality, or common sense, or anything of the sort; it simply means – well, let's show what it means by a couple of examples.

Many centuries ago, the Chinese empress Si Ling-chi overheard complaints that "worms," or moth larvae, were devouring the leaves of the royal mulberry tree. So she went out to see what was happening. She watched the larvae as they spun their cocoons of strong, shimmering threads. Observing their movements as they spun, she conceived of a way to extract the fibers and weave clothing material from them. Her observations and experiments led to the cultivation of what was to become the most highly treasured of all the world's natural fibers – the magical material known as silk.

On returning from a walk about forty years ago, the Swiss engineer George de Mestral found cockleburs clinging to his clothing. Unlike countless other people who have cursed the prickly seedpods, picked them off, and discarded them, he asked himself, "Why do they stick?" Examining them closely, he found that they were covered with tiny hooks, which had become embedded in the loops of his clothing fabric. He wondered if it would be possible to develop fasteners based on a hook-and-loop principle, which would by their nature be more flexible than anything then being used. From his watching and wondering came Vel-cro-from "velvet crochet," or "velvet hook" – fastening systems made from which are now used all over the world, in applications too numerous to mention.

Despite the tired old claim that Necessity is the Mother of Invention, it's usually Observation and

Imagination that deserve the credit. The major portion of useful inventions, knowledge, and achievement has been brought about by curious, childlike, creative observers of the world around them, whose vision is unclouded by judgments of what is "possible" or "impossible," "good" or "bad." The telescope, for example, was invented in principle by some Dutch children playing with defective lenses discarded from the shop of a spectacles maker. They found that when the lenses were held one in front of another – which, of course, *everyone* knew was not supposed to be done – distant objects appeared closer. News of their discovery spread to Italy and to the eager attention of a man named Galileo Galilei . . .

When you see beyond "good" and "bad," you are much better able to recognize and make the most of What's There. For example, when a Bear overeats a bit and gets stuck in your front door . . .

. . . you can use his legs to hang the washing on. And then use the *back* door.

"That's Owl in the next room, isn't it?" I asked. "What's he talking about now?"

"He wants to apply for a job as a radio announcer," said Piglet. "He's practicing on Rabbit."

"Oh? Let's go in and see what he has to say. This should be interesting."

"Ladies and Gentlemen," Owl was proclaiming. "For a truly Malicious treat – "

"That's *delicious*," corrected Rabbit.

"Hello, Owl," I said. "Just what product are you trying to sell, anyway?"

"*Professor Padbury's Shredded Oak*," Owl replied.

"Oh. Professor . . . I beg your pardon – did you say *Oats*, or *Oak*?"

"Oak."

"I see. In that case, you had it right the first time. Malicious."

"And look here, Owl – do you really want to get involved in this business? Promoting products that don't necessarily do anybody any good, making wild claims, and all that?"

"I thought," said Owl, "that with my voice – "

"Yes, your melodious voice. But surely you could do something better with it. This may be no affair of mine, but if I could show you the true nature of advertising . . . I know – let me play you a recording I made when I was an investigative reporter. Ah, here it is. Now, listen to this – I'm interviewing Rasmussen Slick, chairman of the American Tobacco Advertising Council . . ."

"Mr. Slick, many people have pointed out that tobacco advertising today hardly ever shows anyone smoking a cigarette – nor does it show ashtrays, smoke, tobacco ash, and other things people would naturally associate with your product. I'm sure you wouldn't want to show cancer wards and lung operations . . . But aren't those illustrations of clear mountain streams, snowy hillsides, healthy skiers, and so on just a *little* evasive and misleading? What could you say about that?"

"Well, first of all, young man, the American public for many, many years now has been deluged with statements alleging that tobacco is directly responsible for health problems of various kinds. I would like to say that the proof behind such assertions is entirely lacking. What we are attempting to do is merely provide a reasonable counter-balance to such ridiculous claims, and show our product in a better, fairer light. I am proud to say that I have been a cigarette smoker myself for many years now, and I have *never* (cough) suffered in any way because of my habit, which I find pleasant, soothing, and (ahem) relaxing. (*Ahem.*) Nothing, I repeat *nothing* (cough, cough) could be further from the truth (wheeze) than to (COUGH) claim, as so many now are (HACK, HACK, HACK) – say, couldn't we shut that thing off for a while?"

"Well, Owl?"
"Perhaps," said Owl thoughtfully, "I ought to apply for a teaching position at the University."

Perhaps. And then again, perhaps not. We're not so sure that Owl would prove a vital addition to the faculty. For one unfortunate thing about Owl – now that he has so thoughtfully inserted himself into this chapter to provide an example of it – is that he has an Image to maintain. And Maintaining an Image tends to get in the way of seeing What's There. If one can't clearly see What's There, how can one *learn* it? And if one can't learn it, how can one *teach* it?

You may recall what happened when Rabbit found a notice from Christopher Robin saying "GON OUT BACKSON BISY BACKSON," and took it to Owl for his Wise Counsel . . .

Owl took Christopher Robin's notice from Rabbit and looked at it nervously. He could spell his own name WOL, and he could spell Tuesday so that you knew it wasn't Wednesday, and he could read quite comfortably when you weren't looking over his shoulder and saying "Well?" all the time, and he could –

"Well?" said Rabbit.

"Yes," said Owl, looking Wise and Thoughtful. "I see what you mean. Undoubtedly."

"Well?"

"Exactly," said Owl. "Precisely." And he added, after a little thought, "If you had not come to me, I should have come to you."

"Why?" asked Rabbit.

"For that very reason," said Owl, hoping that something helpful would happen soon.

"Yesterday morning," said Rabbit solemnly, "I went to see Christopher Robin. He was out. Pinned on his door was a notice."

"The same notice?"

"A different one. But the meaning was the same. It's very odd."

"Amazing," said Owl, looking at the notice again, and getting, just for a moment, a curious sort of feeling that something had happened to Christopher Robin's back. "What did you do?"

"Nothing."

"The best thing," said Owl wisely.

"Well?" said Rabbit again, as Owl knew he was going to.

"Exactly," said Owl.

For a little while he couldn't think of anything more; and then, all of a sudden, he had an idea.

"Tell me, Rabbit," he said, "the *exact* words of the first notice. This is very important. Everything depends on this. The *exact* words of the *first* notice."

"It was just the same as that one really."

Owl looked at him, and wondered whether to push him off the tree; but, feeling that he could always do it afterwards, he tried once more to find out what they were talking about.

"The exact words, please," he said, as if Rabbit hadn't spoken.

"It just said, 'Gon out. Backson.' Same as this, only this says 'Bisy Backson' too."

Owl gave a great sigh of relief.

"Ah!" said Owl. "*Now* we know where we are."

"Yes, but where's Christopher Robin?" said Rabbit. "That's the point."

Owl looked at the notice again. To one of his education the reading of it was easy. "Gone out, Backson. Bisy, Backson" – just the sort of thing you'd expect to see on a notice.

"It is quite clear what has happened, my dear Rabbit," he said. "Christopher Robin has gone out somewhere with Backson. He and Backson are busy together. Have you seen a Backson anywhere about in the Forest lately?"

As it turned out, Rabbit wasn't any better than Owl at determining the meaning of the notice, because he too has an Image to maintain – an image of Captain-Rabbit-in-charge-of-the-situation, which involves so much rushing about, so much excitement and what-in-the-world, that it leaves him little time to sit down and reflect on what something is.

"Hallo, Pooh," said Rabbit.

"Hallo, Rabbit," said Pooh dreamily.

"Did you make that song up?"

"Well, I sort of made it up," said Pooh. "It isn't Brain," he went on humbly, "because You Know Why, Rabbit; but it comes to me sometimes."

"Ah!" said Rabbit, who never let things come to him, but always went and fetched them. "Well, the point is, have you seen a Spotted or Herbaceous Backson in the Forest, at all?"

"No," said Pooh. "Not a – no," said Pooh. "I saw Tigger just now."

"That's no good."

"No," said Pooh. "I thought it wasn't."

"Have you seen Piglet?"

"Yes," said Pooh. "I suppose *that* isn't any good either?" he asked meekly.

"Well, it depends if he saw anything."

"He saw me," said Pooh.

Rabbit sat down on the ground next to Pooh and, feeling much less important like that, stood up again.

One of the many advantages of seeing Things As They Are is that we can solve problems through observation and deduction. After all, how can we solve problems if we can't first clearly see what they are? And the best time to see them is in the beginning.

Most major difficulties are caused by a failure to observe the minor difficulties that they start out as. "Trouble is easily stopped before it commences," wrote Lao-tse. "Put things in order before chaos occurs." In other words, an ounce of prevention is worth a pound of pesticide. The overwhelming tendency in unobservant industrial society, however, is to ignore small problems until they become enormous – and then panic.

"*Call out the troops! Mad Tyrant Number Twelve is taking over the world! We've got to stop him – even if we have to kill half a million people doing it! Oh, it's simply awful!*" Well, let's see . . . Who sold him his weaponry? We did. Who trained his military forces in the use of it? We did. Who supplied the materials he wanted? We did. Who supported his vicious dictatorship for years because he persecuted our "enemies"? We did. And who ignored his unstable personality, his destruction of anyone who opposed him, and his repeated threats against world order for all that time? We did. So there you are.

What can be just as hard to see as problems-in-the-making is that a good many "problems" aren't really problems to begin with. People who don't see situations for what they are often struggle against difficulties that aren't there and *create* difficulties in the process. Or turn small difficulties into large ones.

Compounding any problem (or nonproblem) is the traditional Western response to difficulties real or imagined: the tendency to see them *emotionally*, perceiving them as threats to one's personal survival – threats that must be fought tooth-and-nail to the bitter end. In the East, such an approach to life is considered rather immature. Overdoing it, you know; wasting energy. Or, as the Chinese saying puts it, "Painting legs on the snake."

So in solving problems, one needs to know if they *are* problems. Is what appears at first to be bad *truly* bad? The following selected Taoist writings show the importance of that question. The first is our streamlined version of a story by Liu An, also known as Huai-nan-tse:

> An old man and his son lived in an abandoned fortress on the side of a hill. Their only possession of value was a horse.
>
> One day, the horse ran away. The neighbors came by to offer sympathy. "That's really bad!" they said. "How do you know?" asked the old man.
>
> The next day, the horse returned, bringing with it several wild horses. The old man and his son shut them all inside the gate. The neighbors hurried over. "That's really good!" they said. "How do you know?" asked the old man.

The following day, the son tried riding one of the wild horses, fell off, and broke his leg. The neighbors came around as soon as they heard the news. "That's really bad!" they said. "How do you know?" asked the old man.

The day after that, the army came through, forcing the local young men into service to fight a faraway battle against the northern barbarians. Many of them would never return. But the son couldn't go, because he'd broken his leg.

The second selection is by Chuang-tse:

Once when Duke Huan was passing by a marsh, a goblin appeared in the road before him. The duke turned to Kuan Chung, who was driving the carriage. "Do you see anything in the road ahead of us?" he asked. "I see nothing," Kuan Chung replied.

By the time the duke returned home, he was speaking incoherently, and had become ill. For several days, he remained in his bed.

An officer named Huang Kao-ao called on the duke. "How could a goblin harm you?" he asked. "You are injuring yourself. If your vital energy is weakened by fears and anxieties, you will become seriously ill."

"But do goblins exist?" asked the duke.

"Yes, they do. By small mountain lakes, you will find the *Li*; around fires, the *Ch'ieh*; in the dust, the *Lei-t'ing*. In low-lying areas of the northeast are the *Pei-a* and the *Wa-lung*. In the north-western lowlands can be found the *I-Yang*. The *Wang-hsiang* live near rivers, the *Hsin* in the hills, the *K'uei* in the mountains, and the *Fang-huang* in wild places. Around marshes can be found the *Wei-t'o*."

"Describe the *Wei-t'o*" said the duke.

"A *Wei-t'o* is as big around as the hub of a carriage wheel, and as tall as the length of an axle. It wears a purple robe and red cap. It hates the sound of passing vehicles, and when it hears one, it claps its hands over its ears. Whoever sees a *Wei-t'o* is destined to become a great ruler."

"That is what I saw!" exclaimed the duke. He sat up and straightened his clothes. He began to laugh. By the end of the day, his illness had vanished.

The third selection also is by Chuang-tse, who uses an event in the difficult life of K'ung Fu-tse to illustrate a Taoist attitude:

The armies of Ch'en and Ts'ai were locked in battle, and K'ung Fu-tse was caught between them. For seven days, he had had nothing to eat but coarse soup. Although much tiredness showed on his face, he spent the time singing and playing his lute.

Outside the house in which he was staying, two disciples discussed the situation. "Twice now the Master has been driven from Lu. He had to run from Wei. In Sung, the very tree beneath which he rested was cut down. In both Shang and Chou, he was faced with the most extreme difficulties. Now here he is between Ch'en and Ts'ai. He could easily be killed or taken prisoner. Yet he plays his lute and sings! What irresponsible behavior!"

Their words were repeated to K'ung Fu-tse, who pushed aside his lute and remarked; "They speak like small men. Call them in, and I will talk to them."

The two disciples entered the room. "Master," said one, "we are concerned about your conduct. It seems very strange, considering that you are presently in great distress."

"Oh, am I?" K'ung Fu-tse replied. "When a man operates in harmony with the Way of Heaven, his teachings cannot help but succeed. When he cuts himself off from the Way of Heaven, his teachings cannot help but fail. Looking within and examining myself, I see that I am acting in harmony with the Way of Heaven. I have the principles with which to overcome the terrible disintegration that I see around me. Yet you say that I am in distress! There may be difficulty at the moment, but I will not lose the Virtue that I possess. It is when the ice and snow are on them that we see the strength of the cypress and the pine. I am grateful for this trouble around me, because it gives me an opportunity to realize how fortunate I am." He turned back to his lute, and played again.

The first disciple began to dance. "I did not realize before how high and deep are the ways of heaven and earth!" the second one exclaimed.

Is "good" necessarily good? Is "bad" necessarily bad? It's considered good to be beautiful, but many people through being beautiful have ruined their lives and the lives of others. It's considered bad to be unattractive, but because of being unattractive, many have come to concern themselves with matters more important than surface appearance and have gone on to make something Special of themselves – in quite a few cases becoming Beautiful in the process. It's considered good to be healthy and strong, but many energetic people lose their health and strength by taking what they have for granted, not knowing what it's like to be old and depleted – and therefore not taking care of themselves – until it's Too Late. It's considered bad to be ill and weak, but many have responded to such conditions by examining their lives and changing their ways of doing things, thereby building up their health and strength to remarkable degrees. Unattractiveness, illness, and weakness have many valuable lessons to teach to those willing to learn from them.

It's considered good to live a long life, but many spend their long lives sitting and complaining, watching television, describing their operations, and retelling for the umpteenth time what Aunt Gertrude said forty years ago. Many Great Achievers died young, yet lived every minute of the time they had. As Chuang-tse pointed out, even death itself may not necessarily be bad:

> How do we know that to cling to life is not an error? Perhaps our fear of its end approaching is like forgetting our way and not knowing how to return home.

> Li Chi was a daughter of the border chieftain Ai Feng. When Duke Hsien claimed her as his wife, she cried until her sleeves were soaked with tears. But after she had come to know the duke and had shared his palace, she laughed at her former fears and sadness. How do we know that the spirits of the dead do not do the same?

Those who dream of feasting may awaken to hunger and sorrow. Those who dream of hunger may, when they awaken, rise and join a hunting party, While they were asleep, they did not realize that they were dreaming. . . . But when they awoke, they knew. Someday will come a great awakening, when we will know this life was like a dream. . . .

These words may seem strange, but many years from now we might meet someone who can explain them, unexpectedly some morning or evening.

In the meantime, we can look clearly at our lives and the life around us, and Live. Before we start crying and praying to the Universe to take away our Trials and Tribulations, we might more closely examine what it has given us. Maybe the "good" things are tests, possibly rather difficult ones at that, and the "bad" things are gifts to help us grow: problems to solve, situations to learn to avoid, habits to change, conditions to accept, lessons to learn, things to transform – all opportunities to find Wisdom, Happiness, and Truth. To quote William Blake:

It is right it should be so;
Man was made for Joy and Woe;
And when this we rightly know,

Thro' the World we safely go.
Joy and Woe are woven fine,
A Clothing for the soul divine.

Hmm. Everyone seems to have left.

"*I'm* still here," said Piglet.
"Oh – so you are."
"I enjoyed the stories."
"That's good."
"They helped me to . . . *reflect* on things."
"Things?" Such as – "
"*Fear.*"
"Oh."
"Well, I'm going out on a walk, to do some thinking. I'll be back in a bit."
"Right you are. Have a pleasant time."

When we see Things As They Are, we find a world of Magic – the world that has been there all along. And we find ourselves wondering how we ever missed it. As Henry David Thoreau wrote:

> What is a course of history or philosophy, or poetry, no matter how well selected, or the best society, or the most admirable routine of life, compared with the discipline of looking always

at what is to be seen? Will you be a reader, a
student merely, or a seer? Read your fate, see what
is before you, and walk on into futurity.

And now, here's a Riddle for Piglet, when he
returns: If "good" is not necessarily good, and "bad"
not necessarily bad, what is "small"?

The Upright Heart

The wind was against them now, and Piglet's ears streamed behind him like banners as he fought his way along, and it seemed hours before he got them into the shelter of the Hundred Acre Wood and they stood up straight again, to listen, a little nervously, to the roaring of the gale among the treetops.

"Supposing a tree fell down, Pooh, when we were underneath it?"

"Supposing it didn't," said Pooh after careful thought.

Piglet was comforted by this, and in a little while they were knocking and ringing very cheerfully at Owl's door.

And now it's time for − what's that squeaking noise?

There's not much you can do
When you're only Very Small . . .
The Great Deeds aren't for you.
They're important
As they can be,
But you can't do those things at all.

"*Piglet?* Whatever in the world − "

"Pooh's been giving me songing lessons," squeaked Piglet.

"Don't you mean *singing* les − oh, well, no, I guess that's right. Songing lessons. Oh, he has, has he?"

"Yes."

"Well, I only hope he realizes what he's unleashed upon an unsuspecting world."

"Hello," said Pooh. "Has Piglet sung you his song?"

"Some of it, at least. He sings awfully high, doesn't he? In the human world, he'd be known as a Countertenor."

"No," said Pooh. "He can count higher than that."

"Higher than what?"

"Ten."

"Who said anything about counting, Pooh?"

"You *said* that Piglet is a count-to-tenner. And *I* said — "

"Yes, yes. What I meant was, he sings high."

"After all," said Pooh, "he's a Very Small Animal."

"Indeed," added Piglet. "You can't expect a pig to sing like *Pooh*. He's a Bearitone."

"Piglet, what an awful joke."

"Joke?" said Pooh. "Where?"

What was I about to say? Oh, yes. Now we come to the power of the Sensitive, the Modest, and the Small — a power that all Piglets have in potential, whether or not they do anything with it. Of all the teachings of East or West, Taoism places the greatest emphasis on that power, which in Taoist writings is personified in its varying aspects as the Child, the Mysterious Female, and the Spirit of the Valley. Significantly, these are also personifications of the Tao itself.

Let's begin our examination of the Sensitive, the Modest, and the Small by considering Sensitivity. In the West, sensitivity is considered a Minus rather than a Plus. ("Oh, you're just too *sensitive!*") But even in denouncing it as something to get rid of, the West acknowledges a little of its tremendous power. For example, it is widely recognized that being negatively sensitive about one's health through worry-imagery and pessimistic self-talk can make and keep one sick. What is not so widely recognized, however, is that being *positively* sensitive about one's health — "listening" to the body, avoiding damaging influences, imagining and directing healing energy, visualizing perfect health, and so on — can make and keep one well, as an increasing number of people are discovering, some of them through curing themselves of "incurable" illnesses.

Sensitivity and skill develop together — as one of them increases in the process of learning something, so does the other. A skilled ballet dancer is aware of his muscles as they stretch and contract, tighten and relax, through exercise, practice, and performance. Applying that sensitivity, he leaps, twirls and lands without apparent effort. A skilled athlete of any sort is aware of just how to move, how to hit or throw a ball in the right way at the right time, how to do this or that in order to score a point. Our last *T'ai Chi Ch'üan* teacher had developed his awareness to such an extent that he would immediately know when anyone was trying to sneak up behind him. In their areas, at least, the masters of any such skills are very sensitive — and therefore very alert. As Chuang-tse wrote:

Those of perfect Virtue cannot be burned by fire,
nor drowned by water. Neither can they be
harmed by heat or cold, nor injured by wild
animals. It is not that they are indifferent – it is
that they discriminate between where they may
safely rest and where they will be in danger.
Watchful in prosperity and adversity, cautious in
their comings and goings, nothing can injure
them.

Nothing, that is, as long as they avoid having tea
in a storm up in a tree at Owl's house . . .

There was a loud cracking noise.

"Look out!" cried Pooh. "Mind the clock! Out
of the way, Piglet! Piglet, I'm falling on you!"

"Help!" cried Piglet.

Pooh's side of the room was slowly tilting
upwards and his chair began sliding down on
Piglet's. The clock slithered gently along the
mantlepiece, collecting vases on the way, until
they all crashed together on to what had once
been the floor, but was now trying to see what it
looked like as a wall. [The portrait of] Uncle
Robert, who was going to be the new hearthrug,
and was bringing the rest of his wall with him as
carpet, met Piglet's chair just as Piglet was
expecting to leave it, and for a little while it

became very difficult to remember which was really the north. Then there was another loud crack . . . Owl's room collected itself feverishly . . . and there was silence.

Well — so Owl's house in the trees is now on Ground Level. *That's* a fine piece of cake.
"Cake?" said Pooh.

The word for Taoist sensitivity is Cooperate. As Lao-tse wrote, "The skilled walker leaves no tracks" — he is sensitive to (and therefore respectful toward) his surroundings and works with the natural laws that govern them. Like a chameleon, he blends in with What's There. And he does this through the awareness that comes from reducing the Ego to nothing. As Chuang-tse put it:

> To him who dwells not in himself, the forms of things reveal themselves as they are. He moves like water, reflects like a mirror, responds like an echo. His lightness makes him seem to disappear. Still as a clear lake, he is harmonious in his relations with those around him, and remains so through profit and loss. He does not precede others, but follows them instead.

"But where's the cake?" asked Pooh.

"Please, Pooh — I'm in the middle of this. Go look in the refrigerator."

"There's nothing in the refrigerator."

"Oh? Well, don't blame *me*."

The Taoist alchemist and herbalist Ko Hung described one of the benefits of nonegotistical awareness: contentment.

> The contented man can be happy with what appears to be useless. He can find worthwhile occupation in forests and mountains. He stays in a small cottage and associates with the simple. He would not exchange his worn clothes for the imperial robes, nor the load on his back for a four-horse carriage. He leaves the jade in the mountain and the pearls in the sea. Wherever he goes, whatever he does, he can be happy — he knows when to stop. He does not pick the brief-blossoming flower; he does not travel the dangerous road. To him, the ten thousand possessions are dust in the wind. He sings as he travels among the green mountains.

> He finds sheltering branches more comforting than red-gated mansions, the plow in his hands more rewarding than the prestige of titles and banners, fresh mountain water more satisfying than the feasts of the wealthy. He acts in true freedom. What can competition for honors mean

to him? What attraction can anxiety and greed possibly hold? Through simplicity he has Tao, and from Tao, everything. He sees the light in the "darkness," the clear in the "cloudy," the speed in the "slowness," the full in the "empty." The cook creating a meal with his own hands has as much honor in his eyes as a famous singer or high official. He has no profits to gain, no salary to lose; no applause, no criticism. When he looks up, it is not in envy. When he looks down, it is not with arrogance. Many look at him, but nobody sees him. Calm and detached, he is free from all danger, a dragon hidden among men.

Hidden. That reminds us of What's-his-name.

In a corner of the room, the table-cloth began to wriggle. Then it wrapped itself into a ball and rolled across the room.

Then it jumped up and down once or twice, and put out two ears.

It rolled across the room again, and unwound itself.

With the reappearance of Piglet, we come to the second admired characteristic we mentioned at the beginning of the chapter: Modesty. Which brings us to one of our favorite selections from the writings of Chuang-tse:

On a trip to Sung, Yang-tse spent the night at an inn. The innkeeper had two wives, one beautiful, the other very plain. The plain one was treated with honor and affection, but the beautiful one was ignored. The next day, Yang-tse asked a boy of the household why. He replied, "The beautiful one knows that she is beautiful; the plain one knows that she is plain."

When Yang-tse returned, he addressed his disciples: "Remember this, my followers. Put away your pride, and act upon your Virtue. If you do this, how can you not be loved?"

As that story so perfectly sums up the subject of Modesty, we think, let's go on to that of the Small.

"Have you anything to say about the Small, Piglet?"

"Why, yes," he replied. "I was just rehearsing it (ahem)."

There's not much you can be
When you're not so very tall,
And the Life you long for
Is so high up
You can't reach it —
You're a Very Small Animal.

What if I could be Bigger, and
What if I could be Tall?
Think what I could accomplish then.
As it is, I'm too small,
Much too small.

"Thank you, Piglet. That's about what I thought you'd say."

To the typical mind of the West, Bigger is Better: The large man is a better fighter than the little man, the huge corporation is superior to the small company, the adult is wiser than the child. The Taoist attitude is: Not so.

Is the large man a better fighter than the little man? Our previously mentioned *T'ai Chi Ch'üan* teacher, a small man even by Chinese standards, was once trapped in a Hong Kong alley by a gang of armed thugs. They lost. In martial arts, as in Real Life, it's not the *big* opponent one needs to watch out for; it's the *little* one. There are many reasons, some physical (lower center of gravity), some mental (tricks learned from being the Underdog), some emotional (without interference from a Muscleman Ego, one can move very fast). Large men tend to be lazy and slow, relying on their muscles to carry them through a situation. Little men tend to be far more energetic, flexible, and alert, with finer-tuned nervous systems and less weight to haul around. We've so often seen small fighters dance around their larger opponents, strike them at will and dance out of range, that we laugh when we're told what a Big Bruiser so-and-so is. What does it matter if he's as big as a boxcar, if he can't catch you? To illustrate what we mean, here's the Chinese story of "The Monkeys and the Grasshoppers":

One day a long time ago, some monkeys who lived on a mountain decided they would rather live in the valley below, where it was warmer. But when they went down to the valley, they were bothered by grasshoppers. So they tried to persuade the grasshoppers to leave, first by coaxing and then by threats. But the grasshoppers refused to go. "You puny creatures!" roared the Head Monkey. "If you won't leave, we'll force you out! Tomorrow we'll fight you to the finish!" "All right," said the Head Grasshopper. "If that's the way you want it."

The next day the monkeys marched into the valley, armed with heavy clubs. "Come out, grasshoppers!" they called. "Where are you?" "Here we are!" answered the grasshoppers, as they leaped onto their opponents. *Whack, whack, whack* went the clubs, as one monkey battered another. The grasshoppers were too fast for them. The Head Monkey found to his disgust that the Head Grasshopper had landed on his nose. "I'll get him, boss!" said the monkey next to him. He struck a ferocious blow with his club, missing the grasshopper (who by then had leaped away) but squashing the Head Monkey's nose deep between his eyes. And so it went with one monkey's nose after another. Finally the monkeys staggered away, and the valley was peaceful once again.

And that is why monkeys avoid the valleys, and why they have squashed noses.

For the second point: *Is* the huge corporation superior to the small company? That sort of Dinosaur Mentality didn't work very well for the dinosaurs in the long run, and it doesn't seem to be working very well for businesses, either, as time goes by.

As we are told in school, the dinosaurs were the most successful creatures on earth – for a while. But geographic and climatic changes eliminated them because they couldn't Adapt, and couldn't compete with the smaller, faster creatures that superceded them. Their most plentiful descendants alive today, scientists tell us, are birds – small, adaptable, and mobile.

For some time now, big companies have been buying smaller companies, only to be bought in turn by giant corporations, which are then bought by multinational conglomerates. The bigger they grow, and the more interdependent they make themselves in the process, the more vulnerable they become. Bigness easily becomes its own worst enemy. As recent events continue to show, it doesn't take all that much to put a large corporation in trouble. And the bigger it is, the harder it will fall. Survival of the Fattest may have been the rule of business prosperity for a while. But it's now being supplanted by the Success of the Small. In search of something new and useful, creative businessmen have begun to study the fighting tactics of the Samurai. They might do better, we think, to read the *Tao Te Ching*: "The hard and mighty shall fall; the flexible and yielding shall survive." Just a thought.

There was a disturbance behind the table in the other corner of the room, and Owl was with them again.

"Ah, Piglet," said Owl, looking very much annoyed; "where's Pooh?"

"I'm not quite sure," said Pooh.

For the final point on Bigger is Better: *Is* the adult wiser than the child? On the individual level, of course, the answer depends on which adult and which child. But beyond that, wisdom is to the Taoist a child's state. Children are born with it; most adults have lost it, or a good deal of it. And those who haven't are, in one way or another, like children. Is it a Mere Coincidence that the Chinese suffix *tse*, which has come to mean "master," literally means *child*? As the Confucianist-yet-surprisingly-Taoist philosopher Meng-tse wrote, "Great man retains child's mind." And, as the following story by Chuang-tse shows, the great man *respects* the child's mind, as well:

Accompanied by six of his wisest men, the Yellow Emperor journeyed to Chu-T'zu Mountain, to speak to the mystic Ta Kuei. In the wilderness of Hsiang Ch'eng, the procession lost its way. After wandering for some time, the men came upon a boy tending horses. "Do you know the way to Chu T'zu Mountain?" they asked him. "I do," the boy replied. "In that case," they said, "would you know where we might find the hidden dwelling of the hermit Ta Kuei?" "Yes," he answered, "I can tell you." "What a fascinating child!" said the emperor to his companions. "He knows this much . . . Let me test him." He stepped from his carriage, and called the boy to him.

"Tell me," said the Yellow Emperor. "If you were in charge of the empire, how would you go about ruling it?"

"I know only the tending of horses," the boy replied. "Is ruling the empire any different from that?"

Not satisfied, the emperor questioned him again:

"I realize that governing is hardly your concern.

Still, I would like to know if you have ever had any thoughts about it."

The boy did not answer. The emperor asked him once more. The boy replied by asking, "Is governing the empire different from tending horses?"

"Explain the tending of horses," said the Yellow Emperor, "and I will tell you."

"When taking care of horses," said the boy, "we make sure that no harm comes to them. In doing so, we put aside anything within ourselves that would injure them. Can ruling a nation differ from that?"

The Yellow Emperor bowed his head twice to the ground. "Heavenly Master!" he exclaimed.

"Does it have pink icing?" asked Pooh.

"Pooh, whatever are you talking about?"

"The *cake*."

"*What* cake?"

"The cake you mentioned. 'A fine piece of cake,' you said."

"Oh, that. That was just an expression."

"Oh."

"Pooh, don't you ever think of anything but your stomach?"

"I hardly ever think about my stomach," said Pooh.

"Well – I'm glad to hear that."

"Mostly, I think about food."

"Well!" said Owl. "This is a nice state of things!"

"What are we going to do, Pooh? Can you think of anything?" asked Piglet.

"Well, I *had* just thought of something," said Pooh. "It was just a little thing I thought of." And he began to sing:

I lay on my chest
And I thought it best
To pretend I was having an evening rest;
I lay on my tum
And I tried to hum
But nothing particular seemed to come.
My face was flat
On the floor, and that
Is all very well for an acrobat;
But it doesn't seem fair
To a Friendly Bear
To stiffen him out with a basket-chair.
And a sort of sqoze
Which grows and grows
Is not too nice for his poor old nose,
And a sort of such
Is much too much
For his neck and his mouth
    and his ears and such.

"That was all," said Pooh.

Owl coughed in an unadmiring sort of way, and said that, if Pooh was sure that *was* all, they could now give their minds to the Problem of Escape.

"Because," said Owl, "we can't go out by what used to be the front door. Something's fallen on it."

Returning to Taoist principles for a moment: When we eliminate interference from the Ego, the energy of the Universal Way can flow through us unimpeded. Which is one reason why Taoists emphasize the importance of being Small, as does Lao-tse in the twenty-eighth chapter of the *Tao Te Ching*:

> *Know the masculine,*
> *But keep to the feminine.*
> *Become a river*
> *To all under heaven.*
> *As a river flows,*
> *Move in constant Virtue;*
> *Return to the infant state.*
>
> *Know the light,*
> *But keep to the shadow.*
> *Become a pattern*
> *To all under heaven.*
> *As a pattern repeats itself,*

Act in constant Virtue;
Return to the beginning.

Know the high,
But keep to the low.
Become a valley
To all under heaven.
As a valley provides in abundance,
Give in constant Virtue;
Return to natural simplicity.

When we work with the Power of the Small, we follow the example of the Way itself, as Lao-tse pointed out in chapter thirty-four:

The Great Way flows everywhere,
To the left and to the right.
The ten thousand things
Depend on it for life.
It nourishes them all,
Holding nothing back.
It accomplishes what needs to be,
But takes no credit.
It clothes and feeds all things,
Yet does not claim
To be their lord.
It asks for nothing in return.

It may be called the Small.

The ten thousand things
Follow it,
Return to it.
Yet it does not claim
To be their lord.
Therefore, it may be called
The Great.

So too the wise may become great,
By becoming small.

Meanwhile, back at Owl's house . . .

"But how else *can* you get out?" asked Piglet
anxiously.

"That is the Problem, Piglet, to which I am asking
Pooh to give his mind."

Pooh sat on the floor which had once been a
wall, and gazed up at the ceiling which had once
been another wall, with a front door in it which
had once been a front door, and tried to give his
mind to it.

"Could you fly up to the letter-box with Piglet
on your back?" he asked.

"No," said Piglet quickly. "He couldn't."

Owl explained about the Necessary Dorsal Muscles. He had explained this to Pooh and Christopher Robin once before, and had been waiting ever since for a chance to do it again, because it is a thing which you can easily explain twice before anybody knows what you are talking about.

"Because you see, Owl, if we could get Piglet into the letter-box, he might squeeze through the place where the letters come, and climb down the tree and run for help."

Piglet said hurriedly that he had been getting bigger lately, and couldn't *possibly*, much as he would like to, and Owl said that he had had his letter-box made bigger lately in case he got bigger letters, so perhaps Piglet *might*, and Piglet said, "But you said the necessary you-know-whats *wouldn't*," and Owl said, "No, they *won't*, so it's no good thinking about it," and Piglet said, "Then we'd better think of something else," and began to at once.

"I've thought up another verse and refrain," said Piglet.
"Oh. All right, how do they go?"
"Like this . . ."

There's not much you can see
When you can't see things at all –
They're too far above your head.
They're for someone
Who is Someone,
Not for someone who is like you . . .

How can I become Bigger?
How can I become Tall?
When will I stop feeling weak, and
When will I stop feeling small?

"That's all very nice, Piglet. I mean as a song. But it's not getting you anywhere, you know."

"What do you mean?" asked Piglet.

"I mean, that attitude won't do you any good. If you keep repeating that sort of thought, you'll just convince yourself that you're powerless. Isn't that why you feel so afraid?"

"Well," said Piglet, "when you're only a Very Small Animal – "

"If I might make a suggestion . . ."

"Yes?"

"First of all, the fears that push *you* about are not legitimate, appropriate responses to What Is, such as warnings of danger ahead. Instead, they're the constricting fantasies of What *If*: 'What if I should meet a Heffalump, or fall on my face, or make an utter fool of myself?' Isn't that true?"

"Yes . . . I suppose so."

"I would suggest that the next time a What If starts badgering you, look it straight in the eyes and ask it, '*All right, what's the very worst that could happen?*' And when it answers, ask yourself, '*What could I do about it?*' You'll find there always will be something. Then you'll see that you can have power in any situation. And when you realize that, the fears will go away."

"They will?"

"Especially when you realize where the power comes from. In one way or another, we're *all* Very Small Animals, and that's all we need to be. So why worry about it? All we have to do is live in harmony with the Way, for the benefit of the world, and let its power work through us. Let *it* do the work."

"Oh," said Piglet.

"For example, I'm not writing this book. That would be Struggle and Difficulty. Instead, I'm letting the book write itself, through me. That's Fun and Excitement. It flows along, and I follow as best I can. Day by day, wherever I go, things come to me and I include them in these pages. To paraphrase my favorite Haiku writer, Matsuo Bashō 'Every bend in the road brings me new ideas; every dawn gives me fresh feelings.' Writing with the Way is a journey. And so is everything else. Who knows where the Way will take us tomorrow, and what it will have us doing?"

"I never thought of it like that," said Piglet.

"So you see, as long as we follow the Way, we won't be intimidated by fears – neither fear of failure nor fear of success."

"Fear of *success*? Is there such a thing?"

"There certainly is, and it has a great deal of power over a great many people. Chuang-tse wrote some things about it. Here's one of them":

> Yao was seeing the sights at Hua when the border guardian recognized him and approached, saying "Ah, Master! Blessings on the Master! May he live long!"
>
> "Hush!" said Yao.
>
> "May the Master have much wealth!"
>
> "Hush!"
>
> "May he have many sons!"
>
> "Hush!"
>
> "How is this?" asked the border guardian. "Long life, much wealth and many sons are what everyone one wishes for. Why do you not want them?"

"Many sons," said Yao, "mean many worries. Much wealth means much trouble. Long life means long suffering of abuse. These interfere with the cultivation of Virtue. That is why I do not want them."

"Before," the border guardian replied, "I thought you were a Master. Now I see you are only a Superior Man. Heaven, in sending you sons, is sure to have fashioned occupations for them. If you had many sons, and they had their occupations, what would you have to worry about? If you had much wealth and shared it with others, what trouble would you have? As for long life . . .

"The wise man finds his dwelling like a quail, without worries or struggle. He is fed like a fledgling, by the all-providing Way of Heaven. He travels through life like a bird in flight, leaving no trace as he passes. When the empire follows the Way, he shares in the prosperity. When it loses the Way, he retires and cultivates his Virtue. After many years of contented living, he leaves this world and rides the white clouds. No evil will have reached him. He is free from misfortune. What abuse has he suffered?" With this the border guardian turned and walked away.

Yao followed him. "Wait!" he called. "I would like to ask — "

"Oh, go away!" replied the border guardian.

"That story," I said, "illustrates what the Taoists mean by 'Treat gain and loss as the same.' They mean don't be Intimidated. Don't make a Big Deal of anything — just accept things as they come to you. The Universe knows what it's doing. So don't develop a big ego, and don't be afraid."

"Oh," said Piglet. "I see."

"Going out?" I asked.

"Yes," he said. "I'm going to work on my song."

"Owl," said Pooh, "I have thought of something."

"Astute and Helpful Bear," said Owl.

Pooh looked proud at being called a stout and helpful bear, and said modestly that he just happened to think of it. You tied a piece of string to Piglet, and you flew up to the letter-box with the other end in your beak, and you pushed it through the wire and brought it down to the floor, and you and Pooh pulled hard at this end, and Piglet went slowly up at the other end. And there you were.

Yes, there you were. Unless, as Owl pointed out, the string should happen to break . . .

"It won't break," whispered Pooh comfortingly, "because you're a Small Animal, and I'll stand underneath, and if you save us all, it will be a Very Grand Thing to talk about afterwards, and perhaps I'll make up a Song, and people will say 'It was so grand what Piglet did that a Respectful Pooh Song was made about it.'"

Piglet felt much better after this, and when everything was ready, and he found himself slowly going up to the ceiling, he was so proud that he would have called out "Look at *me*!" if he hadn't been afraid that Pooh and Owl would let go of their end of the string and look at him.

"Up we go!" said Pooh cheerfully.

"The ascent is proceeding as expected," said Owl helpfully. Soon it was over. Piglet opened the letter-box and climbed in.

Then, having untied himself, he began to squeeze into the slit, through which in the old days when front doors *were* front doors, many an unexpected letter that WOL had written to himself had come slipping.

He squeezed and he squoze, and then with one last sqooze he was out.

And Victory was theirs. And so was Help and Rescue. Which just goes to show —

"Here I am again," said Piglet.
"So you are. Another verse, is it?"
"Yes. And refrain."
"Refrain, too? Good — let's hear them."

There's not much you can say
When others, Big and Tall,
With their great muscular
Strength and all,
Find they can't do what you <u>can</u> do,

And you stand there, not feeling small.
What if I had been bigger, and
What if I had been tall?
Think what I would have missed out on −
Not too small, after all.

"Much better," I said. "A great improvement. Well done, Piglet. All around."

"Thank you," said Piglet, looking a good deal Pinker than before.

"Ah − here are Eeyore and Owl. Come on, everybody − we're off to celebrate Piglet's Brave Escape! I've a table reserved at the Six Pine Trees. We'll have to stop at Kanga's for the others, and then − "

"Will there be cake?" asked Pooh hopefully.

"Yes, I believe that's on the menu. Honey cake."

"With − with pink icing?"

"Yes. And there'll be Haycorn Loaf, and − oh, why *talk* about it? Come on, Piglet, don't lag behind."

"Yes, come along," said Pooh. "And bring the rest of your song."

"I'm coming . . ."

Why should I have been bigger, then?
Why should I have been tall?
Why should I have been different, then,
After all?

The Day of Piglet

They had got a rope and were pulling Owl's chairs and pictures and things out of his old house so as to be ready to put them into his new one. Kanga was down below tying the things on, and calling out to Owl, "You won't want this dirty old dish-cloth any more, will you, and what about this carpet, it's all in holes," and Owl was calling back indignantly, "Of course I do! It's just a question of arranging the furniture properly, and it isn't a dish-cloth, it's my shawl." Every now and then Roo fell in and came back on the rope with the next article, which flustered Kanga a little because she never knew where to look for him. So she got cross with Owl and said that his house was a Disgrace, all damp and dirty, and it was quite time it did tumble down. Look at that horrid bunch of toadstools growing out of the

floor there! So Owl looked down, a little surprised because he didn't know about this, and
then gave a short sarcastic laugh, and explained
that that was his sponge, and that if people didn't
know a perfectly ordinary bath-sponge when
they saw it, things were coming to a pretty pass.
"*Well!*" said Kanga, and Roo fell in quickly,
crying, "I *must* see Owl's sponge! Oh, there it is!
Oh, Owl! Owl, it isn't a sponge, it's a spudge!
Do you know what a spudge is, Owl? It's when
your sponge gets all –" and Kanga said, "Roo,
dear!" very quickly, because that's *not* the way to
talk to anybody who can spell TUESDAY.

Just what is it that Owl's house reminds us of? It
seems so familiar, somehow. Let's go over it as though
it were still standing – perhaps that will help us make
the association. Let's see . . . It looks down on all
around it, as if tempting the forces of the natural world
to knock it over. It has been sliding into disrepair for
quite some time, as its proprietor has neglected its
necessary maintenance for other things. It . . . Oh,
yes – *that's* what it reminds us of: our civilization. Will
it fall down, too? We wish we could say, "I wonder
what will happen to it." But we can't say that, because
we know.

It's intriguing, and rather Eerie sometimes, how
history tends to repeat itself. The Us First, War Lord

Confucianists criticized by Lao-tse and other ancient Taoists seem to have put on new clothes and come back again to take charge. Reading the *Tao Te Ching*'s descriptions of the society of its time, one gets the strangest feeling that they were written the day before yesterday. So once again, Taoism – for all its great age – seems very up-to-the-minute. And once again, perhaps it has something to offer.

Because, we believe, it is not exactly Progress for our nation to have moved from the enlightened era of President John F. Kennedy (was it the Merest Accident that he quoted occasionally from the *Tao Te Ching?*) into an era of scandal-ridden administrations run by Special Interests' Candidates seemingly bent on dismantling our democracy and destroying the nation's land, air, and water in the process, while wrapping themselves in the starry flag of Patriotism. For years now, intelligent, concerned activists have been Out, and self-centered, ignoramus conservatives have been In. And that is not what we'd call the Way of a Healthy Society.

Why these people are called Conservatives is beyond our understanding, as they never seem to *conserve* anything. They don't conserve natural resources. They use them up as quickly as possible. They don't conserve morality and the family, despite much self-righteous boasting to the contrary – boasting that falls rather flat when it comes from those who amass money through commercial enterprises that make a mockery of moral values and put impoverished families, widows, and orphans into the street. They certainly don't conserve *money*. Not taxpayer money, anyway. It would appear that about the only things they do conserve are the very things the human race ought to have discarded long ago: narrow-mindedness, intolerance, coldheartedness, bigotry, *machismo*, and greed.

The Conservatives (being very religious people, they say) believe that "God helps those who help themselves." And so they help themselves to everything they can get their hands on. But don't expect them to help anyone else. And don't expect them to help the earth.

In recent years, for example, our nation's "conservative" leaders have started a war to take Kuwait's oil supply back from Iraq, waging that war by authorizing the bombing of offshore oil rigs (contributing to the largest oil spill in history), goading the opposing forces into igniting 30 percent of Kuwait's oil wells, killing a quarter of a million people (many of them civilians far from any military targets) in what is now known as the most environmentally destructive war in the history of warfare. The bill: 60 billion dollars. They have trashed the energy conservation measures of their predecessors, all but eliminated funding for solar energy research and development, handed the wealthy nuclear power industry a taxpayer-funded boost, pressed for oil drilling in wildlife refuges and coastal waters, refused to authorize the long-overdue and increasingly costly cleanup of toxic waste sites, and so on, and on and on. With wasteful, destructive "leaders" such as these, who needs enemies?

Unfortunately for those of us who would prefer to go on to bigger and better things — such as the advancement of humanity and the assurance of its survival — the great majority of political leaders now in power seem to care for nobody but themselves. And, as in days of old, that means War.

At present, billions of American tax dollars are being spent each year on preparations for war, weapons of war, industries of war — running the nation into unpayable debt while across the country untaxed gang lords cruise about in limousines, drug pushers and psychopaths prey on neglected children, homeless grandmothers push their worldly possessions before them through the streets in shopping carts, and citizens of all ages contract Pistol Fever, shooting themselves and each other with handguns at the rate of sixty-four deaths per day — killing more Americans in two-and-one-half years than did the sixteen-year Vietnam

War (and wounding approximately one hundred thousand others yearly).

The huge-like-us Soviet Union went Broke feeding the military, and we're following close behind. Meanwhile, little Germany and little Japan, who comparatively speaking spend next to nothing on military matters, are beating us in practically every area of endeavor. What do we receive in return for the trillions of dollars that we've handed to the Armed Forces over the past thirty years? Let's see . . . Well, we've been provided with warplanes that don't fly; armored tanks that don't steer; weapons that don't fire . . . No, those don't count. That's what we're told, anyway. Oh, there must be something . . . Ah, yes – half a million tons of hazardous waste per year. The military is the nation's largest producer of it. What good *that* will do us is rather hard to say, however. And toxic waste isn't exactly the sort of thing we can return to the store for a refund.

Of course, that waste is sooner or later bound to leak out. Fourteen thousand four hundred military sites are now officially recognized as toxin-contaminated – the cleanup of which is expected to cost taxpayers over two hundred billion dollars – making the U.S. military the country's leading Earth Abuser. The military now directly manages about twenty-five million acres of public land and "borrows" around eight million more from agencies such as the U.S. Forest Service — which allows one hundred sixty-three military training activities in fifty-seven national forests, involving three million acres. How respectfully do the Armed Forces treat the land they manage? Well . . .

The U.S. Army Corps of Engineers describes Basin F of Colorado's Rocky Mountain Arsenal as "the most contaminated square mile on earth." Thousands of animals and birds have died by drinking or landing in its water. Nevada's "Bravo 20" range is a sixty-four-square-mile moonscape after fifty years of battering. In 1983–1984, water from Stillwater National Wildlife Refuge overflowed into the area and mixed with the chemicals in its bomb craters, then receded back into the refuge — killing seven million fish and thousands of birds. Twenty-three million artillery, tank, and mortar shells have blasted the forests and meadows of Indiana's ninety-square-mile Jefferson Proving Ground. Approximately one-and-one-half million of these rounds have not yet exploded. Many are below the surface, nearly impossible to locate. An expert has stated that to decontaminate the once-unspoiled area, it would be necessary to remove thirty feet of ground using armored bull-dozers — thirty feet down for ninety square miles.

"When the empire follows the Way," wrote Lao-tse, "horses haul wagons of fertilizer through the fields. When the empire loses the Way, horses haul war chariots beyond the city walls." And:

> *I have three treasures,*
> *Which I guard and keep.*
> *The first is compassion.*
> *The second is economy.*
> *The third is humility.*
> *From compassion comes courage.*
> *From economy comes the means*
>   *to be generous.*
> *From humility comes responsible*
>   *leadership.*
> *Today, men have discarded compassion*
> *In order to be bold.*
> *They have abandoned economy*
> *In order to be big spenders.*
> *They have rejected humility*
> *In order to be first.*
> *This is the road to death.*

The Taoist ideal is to rule by "filling stomachs and building bones" — to take care of society from the bottom up. Today's leaders in government, business, and industry "take care of society" by giving more and more money and power to those at the top. And the Buck Stops There. As Lao-tse described the situation:

> *The court is filled with splendor.*
> *The fields are full of weeds.*
> *The granaries are empty.*
> *The powerful wear costly clothing,*
> *Carry sharp swords,*
> *Pamper themselves with lavish food*
> *   and drink,*
> *And possess riches in extravagance.*
> *These are not princes and lords.*
> *They are robber barons.*

Pooh had found Piglet, and they were walking back to the Hundred Acre Wood together.

"Piglet," said Pooh a little shyly, after they had walked for some time without saying anything.

"Yes, Pooh?"

"Do you remember when I said that a Respectful Pooh Song might be written about You Know What?"

"Did you, Pooh?" said Piglet, getting a little pink round the nose. "Oh, yes, I believe you did."

"It's been written, Piglet."

The pink went slowly up Piglet's nose to his ears, and settled there.

"Has it, Pooh?" he asked huskily. "About – about – That Time When? – Do you mean really written?"

"Yes, Piglet."

The tips of Piglet's ears glowed suddenly, and he tried to say something; but even after he had husked once or twice, nothing came out. So Pooh went on.

"There are seven verses in it."

"Seven?" said Piglet as carelessly as he could.

"A*hem*," said a squeaky voice.
"Oh – Piglet."
"Yes. Have you seen Pooh?"
"Not lately. But now that you're here, I'd like to

ask you something: How are you being treated these days?"

"Amazingly well," he replied. "Yesterday, two people asked me for my autograph."

"Ah. Then the news has been getting about."

"Yes — and it's been rather exciting, really."

"And how has *Eeyore* been behaving toward you?"

"I wouldn't know," said Piglet, "as I haven't seen him for some time."

"Well — *that's* an improvement. Pardon me. Poor old Eeyore. I ought to be more tolerant."

"He does have a good deal to worry him," said Piglet. "It's a troublesome sort of thing, being an Eeyore."

"We all have things to worry about," I said. "You've tended to worry quite a bit, yourself. But you took action despite your worries. That's the difference between you and Eeyore. *One* of the differences, anyway."

"Just the same," said Piglet. "We oughtn't be too harsh on Eeyore. I'm sure he'd appreciate a little Kindness."

"I must be running along," he added. "I need to find Pooh. Good-bye."

Well.

"You don't often get *seven* verses in a Hum, do you, Pooh?"

"Never," said Pooh. "I don't suppose it's *ever* been heard of before."

"Do the Others know yet?" asked Piglet, stopping for a moment to pick up a stick and throw it away.

"No," said Pooh. "And I wondered which you would like best. For me to hum it now, or to wait till we find the others, and then hum it to all of you."

Piglet thought for a little.

"I think what I'd like best, Pooh, is I'd like you to hum it to me *now* – and – and *then* to hum it to all of us. Because then Everybody would hear it, but I could say 'Oh, yes, Pooh's told me,' and pretend not to be listening."

If we seem a bit Pigletish at this point, a bit Wary of wholeheartedly endorsing blind optimism in a business-as-usual future, perhaps it's because we live in a nation that with 5 percent of the world's population consumes 25 percent of the world's energy, emits 25 percent of the world's greenhouse-effect-producing gases, yet does not regulate carbon dioxide emissions. While Germany and Japan have for years been reaping the economic benefits of major investments in energy conservation – making Germany's plan the model for the entire European Economic Community – our nation, at ever-increasing cost to the economy, has almost totally ignored such matters and has spent its money on you-know-what.

Yes, we have our doubts about how much love this country truly has for the earth. Doesn't such love begin at home? Yet even a quick glance inside the typical American house and garage would reveal a startling number of anti-earth chemical weapons with which to keep the forces of the natural world at bay. And outside . . . Americans dump sixty-seven million pounds of pesticide onto the nation's lawns each year – more than farmers use to grow the nation's pesticide-laden food. Some of the thirty-four chemicals used in these Lawn Wonders have not been government tested since the 1940s. And the rest may not be particularly safe, either. . . .

If we appear a bit Hesitant to embrace the belief that we can go on behaving in such an irresponsible manner without paying the inevitable price, perhaps it's because we live on a planet on which five to ten species of life are driven to extinction every day, over seventy-five acres of trees are cut every minute, one-third of the land area has become desert, and life-threatening droughts and floods are becoming increasingly common year after year. In Southern Chile, under the emissions-caused hole in the earth's ozone layer – which is four times larger than the United States, and growing – dark glasses, hats, and full clothing in midsummer are becoming commonplace as carcinogenic ultraviolet-B radiation jumps to an estimated 1,000 percent of the pre-hole amount on peak days. In the same area rabbits, sheep, and fish blinded by apparently ultraviolet-ray-induced cataracts are being found in ever-larger numbers.

And so when we hear Big Talk about growing environmental awareness and about man's ability to solve any problem, observing all the while how man continues to treat the earth and its life forms that run, fly, swim, and slither away from him for all their lives are worth – those that aren't rooted in the ground, unable to move – we can't help but wonder Who's Kidding Whom.

Then we go to the natural world, watch, and listen. And it tells us that a Great Storm is rising, and that before long things will become very Interesting – very Interesting, indeed.

We would like to pass along something that we've learned directly from the earth, as well as from Taoists, Tibetan Buddhists, Native Americans, the writings of the prophet Isaiah, and others: A new way of life is coming – one so unlike today's that it would be difficult, if not impossible, to describe in today's terms. We might call it The Day of Piglet.

Before it begins its approach, we'd say to those people who haven't had the inclination or the time to become acquainted with the natural world: Never mind – you'll be getting acquainted with it, anyway. Because over the next few years, the natural world will be coming to *you* (although not necessarily in the way you'd like it to). Perhaps you might benefit by beginning your acquaintance with it now. Just a suggestion.

Here lies a tree which Owl (a bird)
 Was fond of when it stood on end,
 And Owl was talking to a friend
Called Me (in case you hadn't heard)
When something Oo occurred.

For lo! the wind was blusterous
  And flattened out his favourite tree;
  And things looked bad for he and us —
I've never known them wuss.

Then Piglet (PIGLET) thought a thing:
  "Courage!" he said. "There's always hope.
  I want a thinnish piece of rope.
Or, if there isn't any bring
A thickish piece of string."

"Hello, Eeyore," I said. "We were just talking of you."

"Behind my back, of course," replied Eeyore. "Skullduggery and whatnot. One can't know what to expect these days. Even from one's friends. If one *has* friends."

"Stop that nonsense, Eeyore. Of course you have friends. Piglet, for one. He was just now telling me to be Kinder to you, in light of your difficulties."

"He said *that*? Little Piglet said *that*? That fine, upstanding young pig said *that*?"

Well.

But to conclude what we were saying . . . Whether many people realize it yet or not, man, the Inferior

Animal, has by now proved himself incapable of keeping his own species — and others — alive for very much longer. So the earth has begun its own plan to set things right. True to its generous, gentle, and loving spirit, it has been giving us one warning after another of what it will be doing — doing, we wish to emphasize, for the sake of human survival. The sensitive are receiving the messages. But one day when they least expect it, the *in*sensitive will suddenly find themselves Out in the Cold, rather like the mammoths found every now and then up north encased in ice, with once-fresh vegetation in their mouths and an "I say — who just shut off the heat?" look in their eyes. As we understand it, the major cause of What's Coming is the present-day denuding of our planet — the massive overcutting of its forests.

American citizens are spending one billion tax dollars a year to subsidize the U.S. Forest Service's Giant Giveaway of old-growth public forests to the logging industry and Japan, causing countless native animals and birds to lose their homes. By now, ninety-six percent of the nation's original forest has been removed. Meanwhile, the government of China is permanently employing forty-five million people in reforestation, making tree planting a compulsory subject in schools, and decreeing that every Chinese citizen over the age of eleven must plant from three to five trees a year. (The smaller children are being taught to plant grasses and flowers.) Maybe these people Know something.

"Back again, eh? Did you find Pooh?"

"No," replied Piglet. "I don't know *where* he is. Hello, Eeyore."

"Ah," said Eeyore. "Friend Piglet. Not like some around here."

"Eeyore," said I, "have you seen Pooh?"

"Yes. I have. He's a rather short, roundish Bear — pleasant personality, but not particularly intelligent, if you know what I — "

"Yes, yes. But do you know where he *is*?"

"No."

"Oh, here he comes, Piglet — with Rabbit."

"Pooh," asked Piglet, "did you remember to help Owl remove that — "

"Of course," said Pooh. "I have a phonographic memory, you know."

"You mean," said Rabbit, "a *photo*graphic memory."

"No," insisted Pooh. "*Phono*graphic. It goes around and around. Sometimes it gets stuck. That's why I remember things so well."

"So you took care of it," said Piglet.

"Took care of what?" asked Pooh.

Yes. But let's continue, shall we? We'd like to suggest a thing or two that might help us through the previously mentioned Approaching Transition.

As we hope we've shown by now, Taoism is not an Unbending Path. After all, Taoism follows Tao – and Tao does not operate in a rigid, unyielding manner. As Lao-tse emphatically stated in the first line of the *Tao Te Ching*, "The Way that can be followed [literally: "The Way that can be the Way"] is *not* a changeless way" (a line usually translated as "The Way that can be told is not the Eternal Way"). Traditionally, Taoism is considered the Way of the Dragon – the dragon being the Chinese symbol of transformation. Considering the Bad Press that dragons have received in this part of the world, perhaps a better image would be that of the Butterfly. Whatever the symbol used, Taoism is a Way of Transformation – a way through which something is changed into something else.

It is fitting that for centuries Taoists have been associated with magic, as Taoism is, on one level or another, a form of magic — a very *practical* form, perhaps, but magic all the same. Here we will briefly describe two secrets of that magic — two principles of Taoist transformation that may prove Useful in the coming years. The first is Turn the Negative into Positive. The second is Attract Positive with Positive. Unlike some other Taoist secrets, there is little danger of these principles falling into the Wrong Hands; because in the wrong hands, they won't work. We might add that they work best for Piglets.

Turn the Negative into Positive is a principle well known in the Taoist martial arts. Using it for self-defense, you turn your attacker's power to your benefit by deflecting it back at him. In effect, he swings his fist and hits himself in the face. And after a while, if he has any intelligence at all, he stops and leaves you alone.

Transforming negative into positive, you work with whatever comes your way. If others throw bricks at you, build a house. If they throw tomatoes, start a vegetable stand. You can often change a situation simply by changing your attitude toward it. For example, a Traffic Jam can be turned into an Opportunity to Think, or Converse, or Read, or Write a Letter. When we give up our images of self-importance and our ideas of what *should* be, we can help things become what they need to be.

In a similar way, negative personality traits can be transformed. Self-centered stubbornness can be changed into a selfless devotion to an altruistic cause. A desire to control others can be turned into a desire to take control of one's own life and improve oneself – and help others do the same. A tendency to become lost in details can be transformed into the ability to connect things carefully together, step by step, to reach a goal. Indecisiveness can be developed into versatility, and a balanced point of view. And so on.

> *So to the letter-box he rose,*
> *   While Pooh and Owl said "Oh!"*
> *   and "Hum!"*
> *   And where the letters always come*
> *(Called "LETTERS ONLY") Piglet sqoze*
> *His head and then his toes.*

> *O gallant Piglet (PIGLET)! Ho!*
> *   Did Piglet tremble? Did he blinch?*
> *   No, no, he struggled inch by inch*
> *Through LETTERS ONLY, as I know*
> *Because I saw him go.*

The following is one of our favorite examples of someone who turned the negative into positive.

In January 1838, the immensely popular English writer Charles Dickens was in Yorkshire under an assumed name, carrying out a personal investigation of some boarding schools he had been hearing about since his childhood. It didn't take him long to discover that the rumors he'd heard of brutalized unwanted children had been understatements. In an accusation against schoolmaster William Shaw dictated by a pupil who had gone blind in his care, Dickens read that "Supper consisted of warm milk and water and bread. . . . Five boys generally slept in a bed. . . . On Sunday they had pot skimmings for tea, in which there was vermin. . . . There were eighteen boys there beside himself, of whom two were totally blind. . . . In November, he was quite blind and was then sent to a private room where there were nine other boys [gone] blind. . . ."

On a dreary afternoon, with snow covering the ground, Dickens wandered through a Yorkshire cemetery, counting the graves of children who had been turned over to the cheap district "schools." One gravestone read: "Here lie the remains of George Ashton Taylor . . . who died suddenly at Mr. William Shaw's Academy. . . ." Upon reading the inscription, Dickens conceived a character for his next novel — a poor wreck of a boy named Smike, who would be tormented by a vicious schoolmaster and die. That next novel would be *Nicholas Nickleby*, and it would be written to focus attention on the schools Dickens had seen, and – to use his own word for it – to *destroy* them. Within a few years after publication of *Nicholas Nickleby*, public outrage had caused all of the Yorkshire prisons-as-schools to be permanently closed.

Throughout his literary career, Charles Dickens drew upon his dark childhood experiences – shy, impressionable young Charles forced to labor ten hours a day in a rat-infested warehouse, his father imprisoned for debt – to shine light into the shadows of complacent Victorian society, exposing the effects of socially tolerated cruelty and neglect through his "entertainments." For he worked as an entertainer rather than reformer. He was wary of social reformers, as they tended to turn people away from the causes they so seriously championed, thereby unwittingly weakening their own efforts.

Charles Dickens preferred instead to charm his London-centered audience with stories of lightness and humor, creating an atmosphere of warm security in which readers *knew* that all problems would be resolved and goodness would triumph in the end . . . And then into this comforting world-on-paper, he would introduce those whom polite society would prefer to ignore – the poor, the forgotten, the abused, the stepped-on. And a society that had long looked the other way began to give attention to its unfortunates.

Coming from a dreary childhood in a shaky family, in which the father was not much of a father nor the mother much of a mother, Charles Dickens almost single-handedly created through his influence the solid, supportive Victorian family and its most colorful expression, the family Christmas celebration we know today. He was also largely responsible for the modern (but now endangered) belief that childhood is an extremely important time of life, one that deserves honor and protection.

During the Christmas season, Dickens – a skilled amateur conjurer – would entertain the children of his family and friends, transforming a bran box into a guinea pig, pulling a plum pudding from an empty pan, sending coins flying through the air, as the children shrieked with laughter.

Charles Dickens was a conjurer of sorts throughout his life, magically transforming the world around him into something better than it had been before. In doing so he gave hope to the hopeless, especially the lost, defenseless children about whom no one of public influence and power had previously seemed to care. And to them, at least, he was far more than an entertainer. When he died, his grave at Westminster Abbey was visited by thousands of admirers. Among the many floral tributes left at the gravesite were, as his son described them, "small rough bouquets of flowers tied up with pieces of rag."

> *He ran and ran, and then he stood*
> *And shouted, "Help for Owl, a bird*
> *And Pooh, a bear!" until he heard*
> *The others coming through the wood*
> *As quickly as they could.*
>
> *"Help-help and Rescue!" Piglet cried*
> *And showed the others where to go.*
> *Sing ho! for Piglet (PIGLET) ho*
> *And soon the door was opened wide*
> *And we were both outside!*
>
> *Sing ho! for Piglet, ho!*
> *Ho!*

"Hello, Kanga. What have you there?"

"The postman was at my house a short while ago," she said, "and he left this letter for Piglet by mistake."

"He did? That's strange – he's usually here by now. But no delivery, as yet."

"There may not be for some time," she said. "Tigger's run off with the mail sack."

"Oh, he has, has he? By now, my catalogues and bills may be lost in the Hundred Acre Wood. Well, I hope he's made a good job of it."

"I'll seek it out," said Rabbit, taking command of the situation at once. "And Owl — we'll need you to search from the air. Come with me, Eeyore. And Pooh, and Piglet — "

"Piglet stays here," I said. "This letter looks Important."

While Piglet's opening his letter, let's take a look at the principle of Attract Positive with Positive. It may be easier to recognize its power if we first recall its opposite, the Eeyore Effect. If we tell children often enough that they are Clumsy, Ugly, Stupid, or Incapable, they will in time become just that. At some level, the mind accepts and retains repeated statements and beliefs as the truth, even though they may be far from it. The sensitivity of Piglets makes them particularly vulnerable to this sort of influence. But it also makes them more than ordinarily capable of positive transformation. Which is why Taoism emphasizes the cultivation of Piglet qualities, as well as the importance of positive attitudes and values.

"I don't know what to make of this," said Piglet. "Why don't you have a look?"

"This *is* impressive, Piglet. It's from Sandhurst University – Pemberton Q. Throckmorton, M.A., Ph.D., etc."

" 'Piglet, Esq. My Dear Sir: The Board of Regents of Sandhurst University wish me to inform you of their desire to grant you an honorary degree of Brave Animal (B.A.). We should be most pleased if you could be present at the awards ceremony, which shall be held on . . .'

"Piglet, that's wonderful! An honorary degree from Sandhurst! Well, well. Now you'll have something to hang on your wall. I didn't know they did that sort of thing."

Let's see – where were we? Oh, yes.

★ ★ ★

As a basic example of attracting positive with positive, Taoist medicine believes that the secrets of health are found in health. So Taoists study the principles of health and long life – mental and emotional, as well as physical – and work in cooperation with them. In contrast, industrial technology-drugs-and-surgery medicine believes that the secrets of health are found in illness, so it studies disease and death. Consequently, the typical Western hospital is not so much a place for the rehabilitation of the ill and injured as it is a battle-ground on which medical soldiers, armed with the latest, most expensive weapons, wage relentless war against Unhealth.

A similarly negative, warlike approach can be seen at work in the world of business, especially in its Western half. A successful individual appears to succeed because he is Aggressive – he chases after things and gets them. Chances are his positive attitude attracts those things to him and creates opportunities for success to happen. But chances are onlookers see Aggression succeeding, rather than Attitude. So that's what they imitate. And, since aggression attracts more aggression, the want-to-be-successful turn business into Busyness, creating an atmosphere of increasing combativeness and negativity in which relatively few are likely to be successful – and even fewer are likely to be happy.

"*Know the masculine, but keep to the feminine. . . . Return to the infant state.*" "*Children, who play life, discern its true law and relations more clearly than men, who . . . think that they are wiser by experience, that is, by failure.*" "*Great man retains child's mind.*" The great man, we would say, plays like a child and attracts like a woman. His play may be serious and his attraction seem masculine on its surface, but it is childlike and feminine nevertheless.

And that brings us to someone we consider the greatest Piglet of all time, who changed his life and the lives of millions by applying the tremendous power available to those who attract positive with positive. We will introduce him with these words by Chuang-tse:

> If a great master ruled the empire, he would stimulate the minds of the people by working in harmony with them, so they carried out his teachings unconsciously and without rebelling. Under his influence they would reform their manners, the evil and violence within them would be extinguished, and they would move forward as individuals acting for the common good, as if they did so on their own initiative.

> Could such a leader be compared to even the greatest names in recorded history? He would come from a time before any of them existed. His only desire would be to bring other minds to rest in the Virtue of those long-forgotten days.

As a small boy, Mohandas Karamchand Gandhi was frail and shy. "My books and my lessons were my sole companions," he later wrote. "To be at school at the stroke of the hour and to run back home as soon as the school closed — that was my daily habit. I literally ran back, because I could not bear to talk to anybody." For years he would not go out at night. As a young man, he went to England to study law. "Even when I paid a social call," he wrote, "the presence of half a dozen or more people would strike me dumb."

But Mohandas Gandhi was a Learner. He learned from his studies. He learned from being the perpetual Piglet. And from his parents he learned, in time, some of the most important lessons of his life.

From his father he learned the importance of bravery, generosity, and unwavering adherence to the principles of morality and truth. From his mother he learned the importance of gentleness, modesty, and consideration, as well as the flexible strength that enables one to overcome through yielding. From both he learned that if one wants positive results, one must be positive, and that goodness persistently applied will always triumph over evil, even though it may seem to take a good deal of time doing so.

Eventually, through applying what he learned to the advancement of one Underdog Cause after another, Gandhi became known as quite a fighter, winning battles that many older, more experienced campaigners told him could not be won. He not only won them; he did so by, as the Chinese saying puts it, "fighting without fighting."

Encountering massive, statutory discrimination against Indians in South Africa, Gandhi began a campaign of nonviolent resistance. In jail for his respectfully uncompliant behavior, he read and was inspired by Henry David Thoreau's essay "Civil Disobedience." But words like "resistance" and "disobedience"bothered him. Wanting a more positive term, he and a cousin came up with *Satyagraha*, or Truth Power.

Gandhi said that Truth Power would overcome opponents by changing them with respectful, patient persistence — transforming them, not annihilating them. Again and again, he was told it would not work. And again and again, despite overwhelming odds, it did.

In South Africa, Truth Power brought about the Indian Relief Bill. In India, it achieved the granting of democratic reforms; united long-separated political territories, parties, and factions; stopped civil war; revived home industries; freed the nation from British rule; and freed the "untouchables" from the ages-old caste system that had persecuted and imprisoned them. It earned Gandhi — who held no government office, but led India just the same — a popular respect so high that he could exact political concessions by fasting. And it earned for him, despite his strong distaste for it, the title of *Mahatma*, Great Soul. Gandhi insisted that he was no god — the success of *Satyagraha* in his life, he said, showed that anyone could achieve similar results.

Wherever Gandhi went, he transformed situations

and lives. As one friend and biographer wrote, "He . . . changed human beings by regarding them not as what they thought they were but as though they were what they wished to be, and as though the good in them was all of them."

Many descriptions have been written of M.K. Gandhi and his Truth Power movement. But our favorite has never, we believe, been quoted. It was written by Lao-tse centuries before Mohandas Gandhi's birth, in chapter after chapter of the *Tao Te Ching*:

> *Nothing in the world is more yielding and gentle than water. Yet it has no equal for conquering the resistant and tough. The flexible can overcome the unbending; the soft can overcome the hard.*

★   ★   ★

> *Why is the sea the king of ten thousand streams? Because it lies beneath them. Therefore, if the great man would rule the people, he must put himself below them. If he would lead them, he must put himself behind. Then they will neither feel oppressed by his weight nor threatened by his prominence. The world will delight in pushing him forward, and will never tire of him.*

★   ★   ★

> *A good commander does not rush ahead. A good fighter does not show anger. A good conquerer does not*

antagonize. *A good employer does not act superior. This is called "the Virtue of not striving," "making use of the abilities of men," and "matching heaven" — the extreme limit of the ancients.*

★ ★ ★

I am good to those who are good. I am good to those who are not good. And so all attain goodness. I am sincere to the sincere. I am sincere to the insincere. And so all attain sincerity.

★ ★ ★

Fine weapons are instruments of evil. All creatures hate them. Therefore, followers of the Way do not use them. . . . To rejoice over victory by violence is to rejoice over slaughter. He who rejoices over slaughter cannot unite all within the empire. . . . The wise ruler sees a military triumph as a funeral.

★ ★ ★

The violent die violently — that is the foundation of my teaching.

★ ★ ★

Yield and prevail. Bend and be straightened. Empty and be filled. . . . The great man embraces the One, and becomes its model to the empire. Not showing off, he shines. Not asserting himself, he becomes known. Not taking credit, he is acclaimed. Not boasting, he endures. He does not strive against others, so others do not contend with him. The ancients said, "Yield and prevail." Is that a worthless saying? Put it into practice, and all things will come to you.

Many say that Lao-tse's advice to those who would rule (or manage their own lives) is pleasant-sounding but impractical — that in real life it couldn't work. Yet in real life it did work. One might even say it worked miracles. But Mohandas K. Gandhi wouldn't have put it that way, any more than Lao-tse would have. He knew all too well what such "miracles" consist of: the patient, persistent application of the laws of spiritual transformation, especially that of Attract Positive with Positive.

"We're back!" said Pooh.

"*Mission Accomplished*," announced Rabbit.

"And we've quite a surprise for Piglet," said Owl.

"So you have. All this mail — is for *Piglet?*"

"So it is," said Pooh.

"From Admirers," Owl added.

"For *me?*" said Piglet, in a throaty sort of squeak. "I — I don't know what to say."

"Then don't say anything," remarked Eeyore gloomily.

"*Eeyore*," I cautioned. "Remember what Piglet said about — "

"I only meant," explained Eeyore, brightening considerably, "that in cases of this sort, there is nothing one *can* say."

"That's better."

"Especially if one is Exceptionally Modest and Self-Effacing. Like Piglet."

"Much better."

"Or like myself."

"Hmmmmm."

As Taoists have long observed and remarked on, something taken to its extreme turns into its opposite: Extreme *Yang* (masculine) becomes *Yin* (feminine), and so on. The present age of man — an extreme if there ever was one — might well be called the Age of the Warrior. Man against man, man against the earth . . . So, according to the Taoist principle, the coming age will be an Age of the Healer, or something of the sort. But first will come what could be called a Great Purification.

As our planet takes action to cast out its man-made poisons and heal its man-caused wounds, many human inhabitants will no doubt give way to fear. Many will cling to seemingly powerful we're-God's-chosen-people religions, hoping that by so doing they will be saved from the wrath of a Vengeful God (not recognizing that the approaching "vengeance" will in reality be man's own actions coming back at him — and not recognizing that the Infinite Universal Power is far more than the narrow-minded gatekeeper of an exclusive Spiritual Country Club). Many will find themselves in the wrong place at the wrong time, because they did not pay enough attention to what the natural world was telling them. And many will curse the world, and believe that they have been cursed by it.

But in reality we are the most fortunate generation since recorded human history began. For when the necessary cleansing is over, we will witness a magical transformation of the world around us by the forces of the earth. And we will see for ourselves what the ancient Taoists meant by the Age of Perfect Virtue.

When the remains of today's anti-earth civilization have been cleared away, we will find ourselves in the state of paradise that existed before the Great Separation occurred. Man's lesson will have been learned – permanently, without the slightest doubt. The wise leadership and light-handed government described by Lao-tse and practiced by Mohandas Gandhi will be universal. And the Day of Piglet will be here.

Farewell

We have decided to conclude this Taoist Exposition, or Expotition, or whatever-it-is, with three quotations from Here and There. The first is a Buddhist saying, the second is a selection from the writings of Sir Arthur Conan Doyle, and the third is our abbreviated retelling of a story by Hans Christian Andersen. Just trying to be democratic, you know.

"You do like to borrow things, don't you?" said Piglet.

"Yes," added Eeyore. "And he never puts them back."

Anyway, first we have the Buddhist saying:

In the world of truth, there is no East, no West.
Where then is the North, the South? Illusion
makes the world close in. Enlightenment opens
it on every side.

Next, Sherlock Holmes, in "The Naval Treaty":

"There is nothing in which deduction is so
necessary as in religion," said he, leaning with
his back against the shutters. "It can be built up
as an exact science by the reasoner. Our highest
assurance of the goodness of Providence seems
to me to rest in the flowers. All other things, our
powers, our desires, our food, are all really
necessary for our existence in the first instance.
But this rose is an extra. Its smell and its colour
are an embellishment of life, not a condition of
it. It is only goodness which gives extras, and so
I say again that we have much to hope from the
flowers."

And finally, our shortened version of "The
Nightingale":

The emperor of China loved to listen to the
singing of the nightingale, which brought him
great contentment. One day he was presented
with a mechanical bird covered with jewels

and gold. To the emperor's amazement, it sang the nightingale's song with perfect clockwork precision, whenever he wanted it to. It quickly became the sensation of the empire — from peasant children to court officials, everyone (or almost everyone) admired the wonderful bird, which sang perfectly, over and over. Ignored and forgotten, the real bird flew away.

But after some time, the clockwork bird broke down. Without its song to soothe him, the emperor became ill. His condition grew worse, until he was nearly at the point of death. Just then, a nightingale alighted outside the window, and began to sing. His will to live restored, the emperor recovered.

And now, since this *is* his book, Piglet's going to give us all a song.

"Are you ready, Piglet?"

"Yes, I (hep) *think* so (hep!)" said Piglet, hiccuping nervously. "It goes like this . . ."

Let's find a Way
Today
That can take us to tomorrow —
Follow that Way,
A Way like flowing water.

Let's leave
Behind
The things that do not matter,
And turn
Our lives
To a more important chapter.

Let's take the time,
Let's try to find
What real life has to offer.
And maybe then
We'll find again
What we had long forgotten.
Like a friend,
True 'til the end,
It will help us onward.

The sun is high,
The road is wide,
And it starts where we are standing.
No one knows
How far it goes,
For the road is never-ending.

It goes
Away,
Beyond what we have thought of;
It flows
Away,
Away like flowing water.

"Perfect!" I said. "I knew you could do it."
"Have we reached the end?" asked Piglet.
"Yes," I replied. "I suppose so."
"It *seems* to be the end," said Pooh.
"It does. And yet – "
"Yes, Piglet?"
"For me, it also seems like a beginning."

The
Wisdom
of
Pooh

The Prestigious List from Methuen

"The Wisdom of Pooh range proves beyond all reasonable doubt, what even Winnie-the-Pooh's most ardent fans may have hitherto underestimated, yet many will have long suspected; that indeed Pooh is a Bear of Enormous Brain."

Current and forthcoming titles from The Wisdom of Pooh

Pooh on Philosophy

The Tao of Pooh
by Benjamin Hoff

The Te of Piglet
by Benjamin Hoff

Pooh and the Philosophers
by John Tyerman Williams

Pooh and the Ancient Mysteries
by John Tyerman Williams

The Pooh Book of Quotations
Compiled by Brian Sibley

The Pooh Dictionary
by A.R. Melrose

Pooh on Management

Winnie-the-Pooh on Management
by Roger E. Allen

Winnie-the-Pooh on Problem Solving
by Roger E. Allen and Stephen D. Allen

Publishing in April 1998
Winnie-the-Pooh on Management & Problem Solving
in one paperback volume

Publishing in August 1998
Winnie-the-Pooh on Success
by Roger E. Allen and Stephen D. Allen

Pooh on Life

Pooh's Little Fitness Book
Inspired by A.A. Milne

Winnie-the-Pooh's Teatime Cook Book
Inspired by A.A. Milne

Winnie-the-Pooh's Trivia Quiz Book
Inspired by A.A. Milne

Eeyore's Gloomy Little Instruction Book
Inspired by A.A. Milne

Pooh's Little Instruction Book
Inspired by A.A. Milne

Latin Editions

Winnie ille Pu
by Alexander Lenard

Domus Anguli Puensis
by Brian Gerrard Staples

Pooh and the Philosophers
John Tyerman Williams
With original line drawings by E.H. Shepard

This witty and elegant *jeu d'esprit* sets out to prove beyond all reasonable doubt that the whole of Western Philosophy, from the Cosmologists of Ancient Greece to the Existentialists of this century, may be found in *Winnie-the-Pooh* and *The House at Pooh Corner*. It shows how the Great Bear explains and illuminates the most profound ideas of the great thinkers, from Plato, Hume and Kant to Nietzsche, Heidegger and Sartre.

Even Winnnie-the-Pooh's most ardent fans may have hitherto underestimated his cosmic importance; this book will confirm however, once and for all, what many will have long suspected: that Pooh is a Bear of Enormous Brain.

John Tyerman Williams is a Doctor of Philosophy and a former actor and lecturer on theatre, English history and English literature. He lives in Tintagel, Cornwall.

Pooh and the Ancient Mysteries
John Tyerman Williams
With original line drawings by E.H. Shepard

Pooh and the Ancient Mysteries reveals Winnie-the-Pooh as master
of ancient lore and the supreme Magus of the coming of
the Second Millennium. John Tyerman Williams explores
A.A. Milne's classic stories, *Winnie-the-Pooh* and *The House at Pooh
Corner*, to reveal fascinating hidden references to the
Millennium, astrology, alchemy, hermetic philosophy, the
Tarot, the Druids, I Ching, the Qabalah, and finally, the
Female Mysteries which light the way to a Utopian society.

John Tyerman Williams proved in *Pooh and the Philosophers* that
the whole of Western philosophy may be found in the
stories of Winnie-the-Pooh. Now, as we move towards the
end of the 20th century, he goes further to reveal the
hermetic tradition sealed inside a honey jar.

John Tyerman Williams is a Doctor of Philosophy and a former actor and lecturer on theatre, English history and English
literature. He lives in Tintagel, Cornwall, close to the
birthplace of the Arthurian Legends.

Winnie-the-Pooh on Management & Problem Solving
Roger E. Allen and Stephen D. Allen
With original line drawings by E.H. Shepard

Here for the first time, two highly successful books are brought together in the same volume.

Winnie-the-Pooh on Management
Using Milne's much loved stories and characters to illustrate such principles as setting clear objectives, strong leadership, the need for accurate information, good communication and other neglected basics of prudent management, Roger E. Allen offers sensible advice to managers on how to make it to the top of the tree (where the honey is.)

Winnie-the-Pooh on Problem Solving
An approachable and invaluable guide to problem solving in business and personal life. Roger E. Allen and Stephen D. Allen use the well know adventures of Winnie-the-Pooh and his friends to illustrate the unique SOLVE Problem-Solving Method, a step-by-step system of identifying, analysing and resolving problems.

Roger E. Allen and Stephen D. Allen are associates of Allen Associates, a management consulting firm. They live in Washington, USA.

Winnie-the-Pooh on Success
Roger E. Allen and Stephen D. Allen
With original line drawings by E.H. Shepard

Only decades ago the definition of "success" was fairly straightforward: "the attainment of wealth, position and honours and the like." But in these more complicated times, people have all sorts of different ideas about what success means. For Winnie-the-Pooh it is as simple as acquiring more honey; for Piglet it's far more serious: avoiding dangerous Heffalumps.

Pooh on Success sets out to give you the tools you need to be successful. By understanding your own abilities and setting sensible objectives you can attain your special dreams and get the pots of honey you deserve.

Roger E. Allen and Stephen D. Allen are associates of Allen Associates, a management consulting firm. They live in Washington, USA.

The Pooh Book of Quotations
Compiled by Brian Sibley
With original line drawings by E.H. Shepard

Despite being a self-confessed Bear of Very Little Brain,
Winnie-the-Pooh has managed some startling Thoughts and
said some extraordinary Things.

This Very Useful book contains the Collected Thoughts of
Winnie-the-Pooh and his friends from the Hundred Acre
Wood. Here you will find not only Wit and Wisdom, but an
abundance of Useful Information, Sustaining Thoughts,
Remarks and Observations.

Brian Sibley is an author, editor and broadcaster. He has
lectured and written on the subject of Winnie-the-Pooh and
his creators. He has also edited *The Pooh Sketch Book*, a collection
of preparatory pencil sketches by E.H. Shepard for *Winnie-the-Pooh* and *The House at Pooh Corner.*.

Winnie ille Pu
Latin Edition translated by Dr Alexander Lenard
With original line drawings by E.H. Shepard

The full text of A.A. Milne's *Winnie-the-Pooh* translated into Latin.

Who can resist attempting, even with basic school book Latin, to read this rendering of Milne's classic story about 'est optimus ursus mundi' – the best bear in all the world.

Greeted by *Punch*, when it was first published in 1960, as 'A real don's delight'.

Hungarian born Dr Alexander Lenard printed a hundred copies of *Winnie ille Pu*, his Latin translation of A.A. Milne's *Winnie-the-Pooh*, in Sao Paulo, Brazil.
"The parents of good students (of Latin) will buy the book for their children as a gift," wrote Alexander Lenard to publishers to encourage them to publish his book. "The parents of bad students will buy it so their children will develop a liking for Latin. People who have studied Latin will buy it so that they finally have a use for their Latin."

Domus Anguli Puensis
Latin Edition translated by Brian Gerrard Staples
With original line drawings by E.H. Shepard

The full text of A.A. Milne's *The House at Pooh Corner*, translated into Latin.

By representing A.A. Milne's puns, special use of words and all the Hums in a translation that reflects Milne's style, Brian Staples shows how it is possible to use correct and acceptable Latin to very good advantage. This will appeal not only to Latin students, but also to those fond of language and Winnie-the-Pooh.

Here are Pu, Porcellus, Ior, Lepus and Tigris, living happily in the Hundred Acre Wood in the language of Tacitus and Virgil.

Brian Staples translated *The House at Pooh Corner* into Latin when he was recovering from a stroke in 1979. For this work he received The Life After Stroke Award.